2/78

Being Human in Sport

D1224202

Being Human in Sport

DOROTHY J. ALLEN

Associate Professor
Faculty of Physical Education
State University College
Brockport, N.Y.

BRIAN W. FAHEY

Assistant Professor
Department of Health, Physical Education and Recreation
University of New Mexico
Albuquerque, N. Mex.

LEA & FEBIGER • Philadelphia 1977

Library of Congress Cataloging in Publication Data

Allen, Dorothy J
  Being human in sport.

  1. Physical education and training—Philosophy.
I. Fahey, Brian W., joint author. II. Title.
GV342.A47 1977   613.7'01   76-39966
ISBN 0-8121-0580-X

Published in Great Britain by Henry Kimpton Publishers, London
PRINTED IN THE UNITED STATES OF AMERICA

Print number: 3 2 1

PREFACE

Concern for the person with all of his or her human attributes and potentials is rapidly becoming a central focus of inquiry in contemporary human sciences. More and more the interest is in the understanding of health and creativity as the exploration, expression, and realization of human talents. There is a graduabut definite movement throughout the world to understand individual well-being and huanness more fully. The sport experience is one dimension of this central focus of inquiry. Sport is defined broadly for the purpose of this book, and includes all forms of physical activity experiences without assumptions of inherent humanness or nonhumanness but with the potential to be either.

The central theme of this book concerns the structure of humanness as the unique and essential being of the individual, constantly emerging through experience and the actualization of human potential within sport environments. This book is an attempt to expand the traditional boundaries of physical education, to set forth challenges to act, to transcend personal and professional conditions that are often limitations for our own humanness and growth. Each chapter represents an inquiry unique to its author's views. Nevertheless, the divergent views are congruent to each other and supportive of a perspective that places primary importance on the humanness of the individual in the sport experience. This perspective, which is new to many sport environments, assumes an optimistic human awareness that sets one free to be oneself, to create and to grow, and to control one's choices and goals. The ironic and somewhat perplexing thing is that the actualization of one's humanness is such a natural and spontaneous process given the personal and environmental conditions appropriate to such growth. Specifically, the concept of humanness implies that one's behavior is more authentically human when it is revealed in accordance with one's psychobiological uniqueness; such uniqueness must be distinguished from the socially complex ego-self which responds to a different value priority and evaluates behavior on such a base. In order to facilitate experiences in such natural and spontaneous processes, it seems imperative to inquire into conditions and behavioral models that will bring human qualities to full fruition.

Within the phenomenon of humanness, there exist at least two distinct modes of human consciousness. The one mode is the intellectual, rational, and verbal; the other is characterized by intuitive, irrational, and nonverbal dimensions. Humanness seeks a delicate balance between these two modes of experiencing; therefore, in one's inquiry into being human in sport, one cannot separate the more subjective, aesthetic mode from the empirical analysis. Those who would pursue questions of humanness can no longer continue to separate modes of human consciousness. Being human is a fully integrated state requiring fully unified processes of inquiry. Humanness is in some respects a developmental, progressive awareness toward a higher state of consciousness. In the end, it suggests that we are connected to each other, regardless of how divergent our views, ethnic background, and political beliefs might be. Such a relationship exists because we all share a common thread of humanity which is the center of our being.

The chapters in this book introduce the reader to perspectives for being human, increasing levels of consciousness, being one's body, and being one's self. The focus of the writings reflects an academic, a professional, and a personal approach to the study of being human in sport. Such inquiry attends to a multitude of questions: What is the concept of humanness? What is the potential of sport for developing human qualities? What is the nature of the human experience in sport? What are the conditions existing in sport that inhibit natural processes of growth?

We believe this unique book reflects a developing area in the study of physical education. The work is intended for undergraduate and graduate students of physical education, especially those taking introductory courses, or those covering the philosophical and psychosocial aspects of the sport experience. Students and professionals in humanistic and/or educational psychology and participants who wish to pursue personal human experiences in sport will find it interesting, informative, and challenging.

We hope the book will present the reader with a valid perspective within which to study sport by bringing together diverse but congruent views that permit the widest possible array of perspectives. We believe it will assist teachers and researchers by delineating some of the potential dimensions of an analysis of the human perspective in sport. Questions appropriate to each section have been included in the Introductions. Decisions about what to include were based solely on the editors' personal judgments of what it meant to be human in sport, and are the result of our teaching experiences, educational experiences, and personal experiences in sport, all of which led to the development of an attitude about human potential in sport environments. For us, and we believe for the authors also, this book represents a personal effort to humanize sport, such effort being based on a vision and hope for physical education.

We wish to express appreciation to the authors for their thought-provoking ideas and questions, to all the friends and colleagues who supported our efforts by their excitement and their challenging questions, and to Ed Wickland of Lea & Febiger for his faith in the significance of unique and divergent thinking.

The problems that arise when many authors are asked to write in their own way on a common theme are indeed plentiful. Nevertheless, completion of this book brings to fruition the expression of ideas and feelings that appear to be in a stage of completion, but in actuality are still in progress. For us, this book is a "work in progress" which awaits future development and extension by the readers and those participants in sport who feel a commitment to being human in sport.

Brockport, N.Y.   DOROTHY J. ALLEN
Albuquerque, N. Mex.   BRIAN W. FAHEY

CONTRIBUTORS

Bonnie A. Beck
>Instructor and Coordinator of
>   Professional Entity
>State University College
>Brockport, N.Y.

Barbara J. Conry
>Assistant Professor
>Department of Physical Education
>   for Women
>San Jose State University
>San Jose, Calif.

Moshe Feldenkrais
>Private Practice
>Lectures at Tel Aviv
>University

C. Peggy Gazette
>Professor and Chairperson of
>   Women's Physical Education
>Eastern Washington State College
>Cheney, Wash.

Ellen W. Gerber
>Former Associate Professor,
>   Philosophy of Sport and
>   Women in Sport
>University of Massachusetts
>Amherst, Mass.

Bill Harper
>Associate Professor
>Kansas State Teachers College
>Emporia, Kan.

Don Hellison

Associate Professor
Department of Health and
    Physical Education
Portland State University
Portland, Ore.

Margaret Hukill

Administrative Consultant
    in Rehabilitation
State of Ohio
Columbus, Ohio

Sy Kleinman

Professor and Chairperson of
    Graduate Studies
School of Health, Physical
    Education and Recreation
Ohio State University
Columbus, Ohio

Kenneth Ravizza

Assistant Professor
Department of Physical
    Education
State University College
Brockport, N.Y.

Frank Rife

Assistant Professor
Professional Preparation
    Department
University of Massachusetts
Amherst, Mass.

Ginny Studer

Assistant Professor of
    Significance of Experiences
    in Human Movement Focus
State University College
Brockport, N.Y.

Carolyn E. Thomas
Associate Professor
School of Health Education
State University of New York
Buffalo, N.Y.

Charles T. Tart
Associate Professor
Department of Psychology
University of California
Davis, Calif.

CONTENTS

SECTION IV. BEING MY SELF

SECTION I

PERSPECTIVES FOR BEING HUMAN

Chapter 1

Introduction

There is freedom to confront great new possibilities never dreamed of before, to be caught up with an imaginative fascination which leads to discontent, and to pursue a magnificent obsession with the actualization of potential. Human potential is our greatest untapped resource. It seems imperative that persons concerned with the development of human potential, such as those in physical education, sport, and dance, direct their efforts toward finding new ways of facilitating experiences of creativity, freedom, and humanity in physical activity. If life, work, culture, and community are to be experienced as something creative rather than as merely necessary, the power to do so must be found within the individual. This attitude toward self, sport, and education forms the avenue for change and for the exploration of new dimensions of experience and action. If one typically functions in a reduced state but has the potential to transcend it, what are the conditions under which such potential can be fulfilled? Physical activity is one experience that requires one's total involvement of mind, body, and emotions to achieve success and to experience significance; it is perhaps unique as a phenomenon in this respect. The study of human potential in the context of physical activity may provide a wealth of knowledge applicable to other aspects of living. Phenomenological study, which explores the experience of being "turned on" in sport and the experience of self and body in such contexts, may well give additional clues about how education might facilitate one's potential to be motivated in learning, working, and living, in general.

The human perspective adds a qualitative dimension to the study of the individual and physical activity. This dimension allows us to extend our abilities beyond our condition, and thus to develop more fully our human potential. Within this dimension are questions of feeling, meaning, experiencing, and imagining relative to the individual. The chapters in this section begin to define a perspective of all that one is and can become. The imperative is the development of the potential to be human, to understand self and others and to relate to them in human ways, to achieve basic human needs, and to grow.

Ellen Gerber writes on the ontological conditions of being human, outlining five propositions of ethical commitment to self. She sets a challenge to make the commitment to self now rather than tomorrow. This challenge is imperative if one is to be human in sport; thus, the challenge asks the reader to go beyond abstraction and to experience oneself in sport, to open oneself up to oneself, to identify one's defenses, and to find the courage to give up defenses and be oneself.

The process of growing into the best self that one can be is intrinsic learning; however, most persons have specialized in extrinsic learning. Bill Harper identifies the necessity of the intrinsic attitude if one is to be human in sport. He suggests that in the pursuit of being human in sport one must admit to the possibility of participating in sport as free activity. It is possible that playing for self-actualization is subversive in a realistic educational sense; it liberates and strengthens individual autonomy; it accentuates individual differences and is committed to the emergence of the player's unique self. Harper identifies three necessary modes of existence peculiar to the realization of sport as free activity. He continues the imperative to act in the pursuit of the possible. To fully understand sport as free activity suggests action, implies consequences, and necessitates direct experience.

The idea of experience as the basis of knowing sport is significant to being human in sport. Participation with an idea in mind is a significant addition to learning *about* the idea. Don Hellison suggests guidelines for this participation in the process of being human in sport. He identifies the search for self as the goal model in the teaching of physical education, and describes this process of searching for self as one of gaining a sense of personal worth and becoming more aware, more creative and spontaneous. Hellison suggests a model-building process toward greater self-awareness.

Frank Rife challenges the reader to examine the goal of being human in sport through the behavioristic model. He presents ways to utilize concepts and methodologies of both the humanist and behaviorist for helping others and for helping the reader develop better self-control. Self-control is prerequisite to developing the power to change self. Rife assumes that systematic observation and recording of self-behavior increase the capacity for self-awareness, this capacity being a positive factor for increased self-actualization.

Throughout this section, Perspectives for Being Human, commitment and challenge are identified and models for behavior are suggested. For the reader to act is to be free and responsible, thus, necessitating a new consciousness of potential and a change in self-perceptions.

Chapter 2

Commitment to Self

Ellen W. Gerber

> *If I am not for myself,*
> *Who will be for me?*
> *But if I am for myself only,*
> *What am I?*
> *And if not now,*
> *When?*
>
> —Rabbi Hillel

These sage words of Rabbi Hillel direct our attention to the pivotal issues that underlie the ethical aspects of "commitment to self." The quotation is an interesting one, because in the tradition of the rabbinic literature from which it comes it avoids didacticism. Rather than command the reader to behave in a certain way, it raises questions, provokes thoughtful replies, draws the individual into generating a response in an intensely personal way.

This chapter is devoted to an analysis of these three questions. I hope, like the rabbi's statement, that I shall avoid didacticism or any suggestion of normative behavior. The chapter is, in its own way, a personal response which I proffer; it is a sharing of my thinking, an offering of my personal convictions.

IF I AM NOT FOR MYSELF, WHO WILL BE FOR ME?

"If I am not for myself, who will be for me?" At first one is tempted to say: "My friends will be, my family, my lovers—all these people will be for me." But the question's implication goes beyond that easy answer. It suggests, implies ever so subtly, that before others can "be for one," can give support and respect, for instance, the individual must first be for himself or herself. In essence, the question is a comment which might read: "If I am not for myself, then others will not be able to be for me either." In other

7

words, it suggests that as a first condition, one needs a positive acceptance of self before others can accept that same self.

This concept of acceptance of self closely parallels the natural order of things. A baby is known to be self-centered, not only in terms of the fact that he/she directs all his/her attention to filling his/her own needs. The self is also the first level of exploration. Before a baby examines the surrounding environment, he/she examines self. Before a baby interacts in a meaningful way with other people, a baby interacts with self. A young child's play is first with self, later with others. A young child self-tests before testing self in competition with others. In many ways, this process is repeated throughout life; in each new situation we usually like to be sure of ourselves before we commit our ideas or skill or feelings in an interactive way with others.

What does it really mean to be for myself? Or, perhaps a prior question is, what is self? The existentialist explanation, particularly the description of being advanced by Jean-Paul Sartre, offers insight into this question. Sartre describes three dimensions of being: being-in-itself, being-for-itself, and being-for-others. The being-in-itself is the root or radical reality of self. In a sense, it is naive existence without explanation or valuation. The being-for-others is the being presented to and/or observed and experienced by others. The being-for-itself is the being presented to oneself; it is the consciousness of self. Being-for-itself is a mode of being that enables the person to deal with self as if self had an independent existence; it is the self dealing with self. I believe that it is this aspect of self that enables us to choose to be "for self" or against self." This dimension of being makes it ontologically possible to act and react towards self as if self were another. Without this existential possibility, one would have no choice but to be as one is, because one would be blind to self. Thus, one's attitude toward self and the world would be a kind of "here I am, take me or leave me" approach. Therefore, the first proposition of ethical commitment to self is to utilize the inherent capacity of being-for-itself to approach self, to examine self, to evaluate self, and ultimately to affect self.

Analysis of one's own being is not a simple affair. We have marvelous psychological mechanisms that enable us to distort our perceptions of self and make them come out as we would have them to be. This really is what rationalization is all about. But we have a commitment to self that is no less than our commitment to another. It is a commitment to see clearly, to see through the glass not darkly, but face-to-face. It is a commitment to know precisely the parameters of our capabilities. It is a commitment to subject oneself to vigorous scrutiny in a disciplined way. In a sense, it is a commitment to make oneself acceptable to oneself.

There is a second factor connected with the human ontological condition that is crucially significant to the issue of being for oneself. The existentialists insist that humans are ontologically free. Free! It is a magnificent concept in that it suggests the ability to choose for oneself (and to choose oneself), and to transcend all conditions that pressure and impinge on us, if we choose. Like human equality, we are not determined or bound by age or gender, geographical location, social status, economic condition, or ideational systems. We are limited only by our selves, by our own capacities, by our own abilities to cope with the context in which our beings find themselves. (I hasten to add that this is not meant to imply that all contexts are equally supportive or easy to cope with. The strongest, most capable human may be unable to move a mountain; the weakest person may be fortunate in finding only a paper to be pushed.)

Because human beings are ontologically free, we are ultimately responsible for our own selves. Even a child or an infant and all adults are responsible for their own actions. It is a responsibility that is endless, that cannot be given away because it is inherent in the human condition. If there is no escape from freedom and responsibility, then the examination of self must extend to an analysis of the results of being oneself. The behavior, the actions, the thoughts, and the feelings are all extensions of the free self. They are indisputably one's own. So the second proposition of ethical commitment to self is to clearly recognize and accept responsibility for oneself and one's own actions.

There still remains one essential word in the question that begins "if I am not for myself": the word is "for." There are two levels of interpretation of "for" in this sentence. The simpler version might be to consider "for" as opposed to "against." And, in fact, if that were all that was meant, it would be a relatively simple accomplishment. It is hard to be against oneself, to act against one's own interests—though it is by no means impossible. Self-destructiveness is a common psychological phenomenon, but I prefer to think it is not an aspect of the healthy self.

There is another, more important connotation of the word "for." Thus far I have discussed the attitude towards one's own being in a rather neutral analytical manner. But Rabbi Hillel's use of the word suggests not a neutral but a positive stance—not merely an acceptance but an embrace. With the intimacy of our being-for-itself, it is not too much to call this a love of self.

Some persons find it hard to accept themselves, let alone love themselves. They are tangled in social mores that seem to imply that self-love is evil or at best selfish. I believe this arises because of a basic confusion between loving oneself and choosing to act only in accordance with the desires of self. To me, these are distinct phenomena. To be for oneself is the opposite of rejecting oneself. It is the basis of confidence. To have confidence is to enable one to stand freely, in mutual relation to others, without fear and without asking from the other the very affirmation one would deny oneself.

Thus, I view the third proposition of ethical commitment to self as the willingness to be self-affirming or self-loving. And if, in our examination of self, in our acceptance of responsibility for self, we find it difficult to do this, then it seems logical that before we present ourselves to the world we influence ourselves to be that which we would like our selves to be. "And last, I should like to be that which I hope they think I am." That is the last line of a poem I once memorized as a young camp counselor. I have forgotten the author and the rest of the poem also, but I think the line expresses well the point I have been trying to make here.

So, the question "if I am not for myself, who will be for me?" suggests utilizing the inherent capacity of being-for-itself to approach, examine, evaluate, and affect self. It implies the recognition and acceptance of the ultimate responsibility inherent in the ontological freedom of self. And it asks for self-affirmation and -love as a basis for presenting oneself to the world.

IF I AM FOR MYSELF ONLY, WHAT AM I?

"If I am for myself only, what am I?" The question is puzzling, for in a fundamental sense, one cannot be for oneself only. If we turn back for a moment to the three dimensions of being postulated by Sartre, it can be seen that the third aspect was being-for-others. Being-for-others, then, is one of the three fundamental modes of being-in-the-world. It is part of the ontological condition of being human. This means that, like it or not, one appears to others as well as to self. The condition is irrevocable in that there is no way one can be in the world and not appear to others. At first glance, there appears to be no choice involved; in appearing to others we are bound to be perceived by them, to enter their world, to affect their being-in-the-world. However, this situation is similar to the idea that human beings are free to act within a context. We may have no control over the environment in which we find ourselves, but we have complete control over our response to this environment. In the same manner, we recognize the fact of our appearance to others and choose the roles with which we shade and intensify the requisite nominal interaction. These roles affect our being-for-others; they provide a framework through which we are perceived; they tend to highlight certain aspects of self and diminish others.

The question "if I am for myself only, what am I?" must be taken as a whole. One begins to realize that Rabbi Hillel assumes that we choose our roles in the world; "if I am for myself only" I cannot give my usual answers. I cannot say I am a teacher, for the most obvious role of a teacher is the use of self to teach others; I cannot say I am a friend, for to be a friend is to join with another in a mutually helpful relationship; I cannot say I am a mother or father, for mothers and fathers are called upon to care for their children; I cannot say I am a lover, because without affirmation of the other, there is no love; I cannot even claim to be a scholar or writer, because without a mission to communicate my findings and ideas to others, my work is of no use. If I am for myself only, then I am not a teacher, friend, parent, lover, or scholar.

Rabbi Hillel probably did not mean for the reader to seriously ask "What am I?" I believe he meant to make the point that the self cannot be for the self only. By asking "What am I?" he was demonstrating the point that it is an inherent characteristic in human society, as in the human condition, that the self be for others also.

"If I am for myself only," then I have no role in the world. Therefore I am denying my existential freedom by abrogating my responsibility to choose my modes of interacting with others. Not to be for oneself only involves making a deliberate role presentation to the world. Thus the fourth proposition of ethical commitment to self is to accept responsibility for the mode of being-for-others with which we present ourselves to the world.

Furthermore, unless one can contemplate purposely choosing to have a harmful effect, the proposition implies finding roles that ensure that the influence of self will be helpful and positive. As a result, it means doing everything possible to enhance the self that affects the world. This really calls for a fifth proposition of ethical commitment to self, which is to make the self suitable for its chosen roles in the world. This proposition implies the development of positive human qualities such as generosity, integrity, humanness, and loving or caring attitudes; it also implies the acquisition of skills necessary to enact roles effectively as, for example, knowledge of and competence in the areas in which one teaches, coaches, or administers.

"If I am for myself only, what am I?" suggests, then, that in addition to accepting responsibility for myself as self, I accept responsibility for myself as a being-for-others. I endeavor to endow that being-for-others with the qualities and abilities that will affect others in a positive and good way.

IF NOT NOW, WHEN?

"If not now, when?" This is my favorite of the three questions about the self, perhaps because it is the most direct and most demanding one. It insists on an answer and somehow it implies that the answer should be "now."

If one accepts the commitments to self as set forth in the five propositions explicated previously, then one is challenged to take action. The self is not to be put off. The commitments to self take precedence over all other commitments precisely because they are the basis for all such relationships. As Polonius said to Laertes, "to thine own self be true, and it will follow as the night the day, thou canst not then be false to any man."

To say that tomorrow I will examine the motives for my actions is to admit that today I prefer to act without evaluation. To say that tomorrow I will accept responsibility for my actions is to imply that today I may agree to assign to others the real accountability for what I myself have done. To say that tomorrow I will affirm myself and approach the world in the full confidence of that self-love is to admit that today I am insecure and nonaccepting of my own capacities and abilities. To say that tomorrow I will accept responsibility for the self that I present to the world is to say that today I do not care that I have an effect on others, that my presence alters their world. To say that tomorrow I will seek to make myself capable of exerting a more effective, more positive influence is to say that today I do not care about the quality of my influence.

To say "tomorrow" is to admit, I think, that one has not accepted the ethical commitment to self. I really believe that it is like giving up smoking or drinking, or going on a diet, or, more positively, accepting and/or loving another person or God. To say that one will do any of these things tomorrow is to say that one is not yet ready to do them. Once one actually adopts a personal commitment to anything, it becomes logically absurd to put the commitment off until tomorrow.

CONCLUDING COMMENTS

Some of us have been conditioned to believe that selfishness and selflessness are polar opposites—the one negative and the other positive. This is unfortunate, for in the most fundamental sense, as I hope I have demonstrated in this chapter, they are dependent upon each other—in fact, may be one and the same in the manner of a Zen riddle.

Although I have examined each question separately for the purpose of analysis, the quotation from Rabbi Hillel must be understood as a whole, even as we have learned that we cannot ever deal with the mind or body as a single entity. The three questions are interrelated, and as such, set before us a unitary basis for our ethical commitment to self.

> *If I am not for myself,*
> *Who will be for me?*
> *But if I am for myself only,*
> *What am I?*
> *And if not now,*
> *When?*

Chapter 3

Sport: Ars Liberalis?

Bill Harper

Sport is usually less barbaric than war, commonly more public than sex, and about as ethical as any other human engagement. It may even be a rather nice thing. And it is truly a good thing to know what things are nice in this world, as well as why nice things are nice. Yet, even though it is true that sport is usually nicely thought of, it is likewise true that it is usually scarcely thought of.

As ubiquitous as sport is, we really ought to be ashamed we do not know more about it. Of course, it may be that the general lack of a comprehensive theory of sport can be traced to some great wisdom about it. Perhaps, as the Tao Te Ching points out, "Those who know do not talk and talkers do not know." It may also be the case that, especially in matters of heart and will (which sport seems to be), there may be no good point in seeking guidance from head and idea. After all, as e. e. cummings reminds us, ". . . (and birds sing sweeter than books tell how). . . ."

I suspect, however, that with sport it is not that we know and do not talk. It is also not the case that we are wise enough to believe that sport is better than books tell why. Rather, sport is simply thought to be not very important—even to be wise about. The lot of man being what it is, theorizing about what is unnecessary, like sport, is presumed to be unnecessary.

What is unnecessary, however, is not always unimportant. Indeed, most of man's creative and imaginative pursuits are, by most standards, not necessary at all. Nonetheless, they are still enthusiastically taken up, usually resulting in an experience of personal, if not universal, significance. Sport may be one example of an unnecessary but not thereby unimportant activity.

There is a relatively quiet dispute that, if blown out of proportion will serve well as a starting point. You may remember the original work of Johan Huizinga in 1938 called *Homo Ludens*. In that work you will recall, Huizinga described play as the sustaining and ever-present constant in all cultural processes and many forms of social life. Among other characteristics, Huizinga found play to be a "free activity" (which was, of course, further qualified). Some 25 years later in 1963, Josef Pieper, in a small work called *In Tune With the World,* said, in effect, "bosh!" to Huizinga's conclusion that "all is play." In his study of festivity, Pieper refused to allow festivity to be subsumed as a form of the larger category, play. Pieper demands that for something to be a free activity *(ars liberalis)* as against some kind of useful work *(artes serviles),* it must be a meaningful activity in itself. Play, according to Pieper, does not satisfy this distinguishing feature of free activity. Human acts, Pieper believes, get their meaning from their object, their content, their "what." And play is not something one does (a what), but the modus of action, the way one does it. Therefore, he concludes, play cannot be a free activity because it is not an activity at all.

Aside from the particulars of whether or not these two thinkers actually differ, the question of the accuracy of Pieper or Huizinga, and the legitimacy of Pieper's willingness to divide acts into those largely utilitarian and those serving no purpose beyond themselves, we shall instead appropriate a common phrase between them. Both essays center on the necessity for and importance of what they call free activity.

It appears that insofar as we have presented the alleged difference between our two hunters of ideas neither has returned empty-handed. What may help us is to pool their "catch." For it seems that free activity *(ars liberalis)* cannot be exclusively either a what (a content in Huizinga's terms) or a modus of action (a way in Pieper's terms). Rather, free activity, to be the intrinsically meaningful action it is supposed to be, demands both the what *and* the how. Neither the what nor the how alone can account for the nature and significance of free activity, which is so rare and therefore precious to mankind.

Although admittedly a bit reckless, I shall call the common denominator "free activity," or play. And furthermore, if there is some degree of propriety in this move, then it further behooves me to suggest that the how of such free activity is the playing of it (free), that is, with what attitude one plays or engages in it, and the what of such free activity is the thing played (activity).

Sport, to be considered *ars liberalis,* must then display two aspects—the playing and the played. It is all too often assumed that because the played sporting activity is unnecessary and done for its own sake, there is thereby an *ars liberalis* brought into existence. But just as necessary to sport as *ars liberalis* is the spirit of the undertaking—the playing of it. The stiffening of sport, to which

Huizinga made reference (owing in part to the "pitch of technical organization and scientific thoroughness," as well as the increasing systematization and regimentation), is nothing more than the played without playing.

In what remains of this brief look at sports as *ars liberalis*, I will concentrate on the elusive and perhaps out-of-season aspect of *ars liberalis*—the playing. Roughly, there are at least three characteristics: (1) choosing, (2) minding, and (3) pursuing.

In *The Adventures of Tom Sawyer*, as you will remember, Aunt Polly expected Tom to whitewash "thirty yards of board fence nine feet high" on one beautiful but hot summer Saturday. Not only did Tom manage to hoodwink Ben and other unsuspecting youths into doing it (three coats no less!) for him, he even managed to get rich in the process. Before the afternoon was over Tom had traded the boring task of whitewashing the fence for, among other things, a kite "in good repair," a dead rat and a string to swing it with, twelve marbles, a key that would not unlock anything, a couple of tadpoles, six firecrackers, a kitten with only one eye, a dog collar (but no dog), four pieces of orange peel, and a dilapidated old window sash.

Tom had turned what was an empty burden for himself into a meaningful action for his friends. And all he did in his "slaughter of innocents" was to pretend that whitewashing the fence on a bright and fresh Saturday was not a chore but a privilege. Had he been a wise philosopher, says Twain, he would have concluded from his discovery that

> *Work consists of whatever*
> *a body is obliged to do, and*
> *that Play consists of whatever*
> *a body is not obliged to do.*

Tom has introduced us to the first characteristic of the free act. Certainly it is not a profound statement, but necessary nevertheless. When the various ways people get themselves into doing what they do are considered, it is still important to remember the place of choice in the scheme of things. It was Ortega who reminded us that life is given to us empty, and "whether we like it or not we have to fill it on our own." Much of what we do to fill it does not, however, result from our having chosen to do what we do. There are all kinds of duties and obligations, some self-imposed, others pressed on us from without. Frequently, after we have arranged the sequence of events in our lives on the spur of necessity, duty, or whatever, we find ourselves all "topped up," that is, filled with not enough room in our lives for things other than duty, necessity, obligations, and the like, so to speak. What we think we have gotten into by choice is merely a result of a course of things over which we exert little control. Choosing freely is simply not altogether that common. Nevertheless, choosing freely is necessary as the first step in realizing the *ars liberalis*.

Another necessary mode of existence peculiar to realizing the *ars liberalis* is what we call "minding." The term is not altogether satisfactory, but it will do for our purposes. Just think for a moment about the way you carry out those things you would rather not do. Like Tom Sawyer before he became wise, we commonly find such things an empty burden. Accordingly, it is usual while we are doing an unwanted task to wish we were not. Our mind is often "elsewhere." There is a lack of commitment which shows up as daydreaming. If we cannot get out of doing it, we at least manage not to allow all of our powers to become involved. If a chore can be done routinely, then we can escape complete engrossment in it by directing our thoughts toward something else. We think of all kinds of other things, such as planning what we will do in the future, remembering things in the past, dreaming of a loved one, solving some problem, and so on. In short, the general boredom of such chores invites our thoughts to be absent from them, to be otherwise occupied or busied.

With the *ars liberalis*, there is no such schism between the activity and our relative attention to it. We are minding it. Instead of time weighing on us, time flies as they say. In those immortal moments, instead of consciousness of a division, there is consciousness of unity. We pay attention. We bring the sum total of our faculties into play. And so our thoughts, instead of being elsewhere, are fully absorbed in the project at hand. We are absorbed in it, swallowed up.

Perhaps Saint-Exupéry in *The Little Prince* put this idea much better. You will remember that among the many adventures of the little prince he meets a railway switchman.

> "What do you do here?" the little prince asked.
> "I sort out travelers, in bundles of a thousand," said the switchman. "I send off the trains that carry them: now to the right, now to the left."
> And a brilliantly lighted express train shook the switchman's cabin as it rushed by with a roar like thunder.
> "They are in a great hurry," said the little prince. "What are they looking for?"

"*Not even the locomotive engineer knows that,*"
said the switchman.
    And a second brilliantly lighted express thun-
dered by, in the opposite direction.
    "*Are they coming back already?*" *demanded the*
little prince.
    "*These are not the same ones,*" *said the switch-*
man. "*It is an exchange.*"
    "*Were they not satisfied where they were?*" *asked*
the little prince.
    "*No one is ever satisfied where he is,*" *said the*
switchman.
    And they heard the roaring thunder of a third
brilliantly lighted express.
    "*Are they pursuing the first travelers?*" *de-*
manded the little prince.
    "*They are pursuing nothing at all,*" *said the*
switchman. "*They are asleep in there, or if they are*
not asleep they are yawning. Only the children are
flattening their noses against the windowpanes."
    "*Only the children know what they are looking*
for," *said the little prince.* "*They waste their time*
over a rag doll and it becomes very important to
them; and if anybody takes it away from them they
cry . . ."
    "*They are lucky,*" *the switchman said.*

Like the children in the express train, players are "flattening their noses against the windowpanes." In the *ars liberalis* one rarely yawns. There is simply no time for it.

In addition to choosing and minding, the *ars liberalis* includes the notion of pursuing. In playing there is a pursuit of the possible. Now this concept is probably nothing more than a reintroduction of what Karl Groos called, over 75 years ago, the joy in being a cause. Nonetheless, it seems appropriate to update it a bit.

Our world is not one in which a going beyond the everyday is made easy. If we are suffering from anything today, it must be a good strong case of lost initiative. The typical human being, if conscious at all of his condition, often feels a desperate kind of helplessness. It is, of course, manifested differently among persons, some being inclined to laziness, others to resignation, others to skepticism, and still others to cynicism. But in the main, it seems that every day of our lives we are being told that we, as individuals, are powerless to do much of anything that really matters. Whatever really needs doing, it is thought, will be done in good time by the various associations of which we are all members in good standing. These abstract associations, alliances, unions, societies, committees, departments, agencies, foundations, corporations, services, parties, bureaus, brotherhoods, councils, federations, coalitions, leagues, ad infinitum, have contributed to our having lost our confidence in our own individual thinking and acting. As the number of our membership cards is multiplied, our individual initiative is divided; as our organization "initials" (e.g., AMA) are propounded, our own individual initials (e.g., W.A.H.) are forgotten.

In pursuit of the possible, such as one finds in the playing of the *ars liberalis*, each human being becomes an originator. Finding himself in a frontier land of sorts, the player is free to pursue to the limits his skill, creativity, and discipline. Even in something like sport, which is often so regulation-bound either with man-made rule or with natural law, there is opportunity for discovering one's boundries within these imposed limits. In such a seeking after the "what can I do or be," we implicitly find as well a pursuit after the meaning of life. And lost initiative is once again reborn.

In my attempt to reconcile the alleged differences between Huizinga and Pieper on the nature of free activity, *ars liberalis*, I have taken the liberty to call such an experience play. Furthermore, I have distinguished two aspects of play: the playing (the how) and the played (the what). Now, insofar as sport can be an illustrative example of *ars liberalis*, it helped to focus on the playing aspect of free activity rather than on the played aspect, because it is usually taken for granted that if one is in sport—being an unnecessary activity itself—one is thereby engaged in *ars liberalis*. I chose to show, however, that if sport is to qualify as free activity, it must also admit of the possibility of playing it, and playing is characterized by at least three components: choosing, minding and pursuing.

Whatever the wisdom of the ages reveals the nature and significance of sport to be, it seems that any theory would be incomplete if it did not consider sport to be, in principle, an illustrative example of *ars liberalis*. But, of course, it is sadly the case that the sport experience as it is displayed in our age is shifting, for one reason or another, toward the bondage of the *artes serviles*. Were sport actually realized to be the *ars liberalis* it could be, the sport experience would indeed be a gate to the root of the world.

Chapter 4

Teaching Physical Education and the Search for Self

Don Hellison

GOALS AND IMAGES

Whether the act of teaching is primarily intentional[4] and scientific,[21] or largely intuitive, inexplicable,[11] subjective,[5] and unique is a question being asked and answered with increasing regularity in the wake of competency-based teacher education programs. It is my judgment, based on my own conscious experience as well as empirical observations, that the teaching act is a combination of artistry—difficult to define precisely and often unintentional—and specifically planned strategies. Whether a particular teacher is evaluated favorably or not depends on a comparison of the teacher's artistry and strategies toward a specific goal model. I am not suggesting that the art of teaching can be measured objectively (shades of behavioral objectives!) only that it is impossible to pass judgment on an act of teaching without some reference point. Specific goal models have not enjoyed clear distinction in physical education, probably because physical educators have tried to be everything to everyone in an effort to elevate status.[20] Regardless of this, most of us can be pegged by our teacher behavior toward a specific goal model, usually information processing (the acquisition of skills and knowledges), but sometimes social interaction (social development and improved social relations), or, more rarely, the search for self (self-esteem, self-actualization, self-understanding).[22] I find myself primarily involved in the search for self (my own as well as my students'), and it is from this perspective that I would like to approach the artistry and strategies in teaching physical education.

   In order to discuss the search for self as a goal model for teaching physical education, it is first necessary to specify my assumptions about the self as the object of this search. My concept of self reduces (artificially of course) the complexities of humanity to four dimensions: a need to feel competent, a self-awareness capacity, a creative, spontaneous capacity, and a uniquely subjective belief system.

The need to feel competent provides a base of support for all else that happens in physical education; if this basic need is not met, students will either "shut down" or spend their entire "physical education life" struggling to, or rationalizing to, enhance their feelings of competence. The conscious self-awareness capacity can be defined as the ability to choose from among alternatives, to reflect on one's own behavior, to truly rise above one's own experiences. This capacity no doubt requires stages of development for full realization.[7] The creative capacity refers both to the conscious creative act—still a subject of debate—and to behavior that arises "spontaneously in human beings as an expression of their inner nature,"[24] including love, joy, and a sense of freedom. Underlying these three dimensions is each individual's uniquely subjective belief system about the self and the world. I agree with Polanyi that reality is perceived subjectively,[16,17] and with Combs and Snygg that the self is perceived subjectively as well.[6]

THE TEACHER–STUDENT RELATIONSHIP

More important than specific strategies designed to connect this image of man to the search for self in physical education is the art of teaching which, for this goal model, resides in the teacher–student relationship. Teachers who are able to develop relationships such as I am going to describe often operate from an obscure goal model, but almost unintentionally get the kinds of results that some of the most deliberate planners and methods experts cannot seem to achieve. This is not to say that intentionality—analysis, planning, and the like—is unimportant in the teaching act. To the contrary, the teacher who can select goals and methods that fit his strengths, personality, and background no doubt increases his effectiveness.[5] However, I agree with Patterson that "the person of the teacher is more important than the method,"[15] that deliberately engineering a compatibility among goals, methods, and the person of the teacher is no substitute for certain characteristics in the teacher–student relationship.

The characteristics to which I refer have a distinct psychotherapeutic ring, a bias that should come as no surprise given my adoption of the search for self goal model. Oden has reviewed the research literature on effective psychotherapy, and has concluded that a "therapeutic triad" repeatedly emerges in a wide variety of therapeutic contexts, for a wide variety of therapists and counselors regardless of training, and for a wide variety of clients and patients.[14] This therapeutic triad consists of nonpossessive warmth, empathic capacity, and genuineness. Nonpossessive warmth—the love component of the therapeutic triad—means caring in a communicative way about the student as a person and a unique human being. The nonpossessive quality implies a healthy acceptance of one's self, that is, the teacher's need to feel competent must be met so that attention can be turned away from self and toward students. Empathic capacity refers to the teacher's ability to be sensitive to the perceptions and feelings of each student, the ability to put one's self in the student's shoes and perceive and feel what the student perceives and feels. It must be understood that this kind of understanding is never completely successful except in an occasional "complete emotional and personal communion" experience;[18] no one can fully exchange places with any student. Genuineness involves being open and authentic and truly one's self with students, not by projecting blame and condemnation onto students but by expressing one's own feelings.[15] Several myths about teacher behavior stand in the way of genuineness.[15] For example, the myth of calmness states that teachers should be calm, even though many of us do not want to behave calmly all the time. The "I treat all children alike" myth and the "I have no favorites" myth require the impossible by trying to equalize all teacher–student relationships.

A fourth characteristic—personal attraction (charisma?)—may be necessary in order for the student to value the relationship with the teacher. On the other hand, the therapeutic triad may encompass or obliterate the need for personal attraction. In physical education, the perceived physical prowess of the teacher may be a personal attraction factor in the relationship, at least to the extent that relating in a warm, empathic, genuine way with a teacher who possesses valued physical abilities encourages the search for self in a physical education setting.

The bridge between my image of man and the search for self in physical education is buttressed considerably by the therapeutic triad. First, the need to feel competent, based as it is on subjective self-perceptions (the private belief system about one's self), seems most likely to respond to a relationship characterized by empathy, nonpossessive warmth, and genuineness, because all these characteristics communicate a sense of personal worth which is not guaranteed by specific strategies. Second, such a relationship paves the way for a self-discovery dialogue between student and teacher which encompasses both self-awareness and the creative capacity. This kind of search may lead the student inside himself to a free act of choosing or even to a truly creative act, a search that cannot be predicted and should not be controlled (except to restrict those alternatives destructive to others), but rather that should be nurtured by a dialogue based on the therapeutic triad.

FEELING COMPETENT

Beyond the teacher–student relationship, a few specific strategies may be employed to facilitate the search for self. About the need to feel competent, perceived physical competence can perhaps be enhanced by stressing self-improvement and intrinsic motivation, by leaving participation in traditional zero-sum games with their extrinsic regard systems as an option,[7a] by providing private places to practice or try out something new,[13] by reducing unnecessary rules, by eliminating written tests for students who have not experienced much success in school, and by grading entirely on participation and effort or on student goal-setting and self-evaluation. Uniform requirements and mandatory group showers may underscore a student's perception of his body as too fat or too skinny or malformed, but these pressures can be reduced by reworking (or relaxing) uniform ("bring something from home to change into") and shower policies. Various forms of individual instruction such as task cards, contracts, learning packets, and the open gym—although primarily aspects of the information-processing goal model—also may contribute to students' feelings of success in learning.

THE CREATIVE CAPACITY

In planning a program, the effort to achieve some balance between methods designed to enhance the self-awareness capacity and those intended to encourage creativity and spontaneity is usually met with a sense of frustration, because the separation is artificial and mutually exclusive. However, such a division allows for intentionality in the teaching act (to the extent that teaching is an intentional act), and should reduce the tension in planning for seemingly opposing capacities. Locke has suggested that about half of class time be devoted to more spontaneous activities,[11] a guideline that can be easily altered to fit the situation.

The time spent in creative, spontaneous activities should not be confused with rolling out the ball—a structured play experience characterized by few, if any, options. Time set aside to encourage this capacity must allow for play, relating to one another, exploration, choice, and the chance to develop new ways of doing things or even a new game. Even if the program is limited to one sport, there are different degrees of competition and play to experience, as well as new things to try inside and outside of game situations. Specific encouragement to do these things and an exploratory environment within a specific time framework, for example, one or two days a week (call it "freaking out" time) are strategies that appear to hold considerable potential for developing creativity and experiencing freedom, joy, spontaneity, and perhaps even love in physical education.

SELF-AWARENESS

My emphasis, to this point, has been on a teacher–student relationship that encourages feelings of self-worth and growth toward self-awareness and creative, spontaneous acts, and on some strategies to meet the need to feel competent and the creative capacity. From the search for self-perspective, considerable class time should also be devoted to strategies designed to enhance self-awareness. For me, self-awareness means working out one's own identity in a conscious, reflective way by building a personal model of desired behavior in relation to one's own needs, abilities, interests, goals, values, and the like, and then by changing one's behavior to match this model. This kind of model-building is idiographic rather than nomothetic in the sense that evaluations are made by comparing the person's behavior with his personal model or by relating various aspects of the model to each other, not by comparing models or abstracting traits from models for comparison.[20]

Model-building cannot take place without talking with students, something we might call "self-awareness education." Self-awareness education refers to the teacher's efforts to encourage students to take charge of their own lives, to take this opportunity in physical education to search for self. Talking with students about something other than skills, rules, and strategies has not been characteristic of physical education, although it was advocated over 40 years ago.[8] As Brewster Smith has suggested, if a person perceives himself to be a pawn manipulated by his environment, he will probably behave that way, whereas a person who perceives himself to be an agent of change in his own life is more likely to behave according to this perception.[23] Self-awareness education cannot meet the need to feel competent, although it can foster an understanding of that need as it operates in physical education. It cannot substitute for the exploring and choosing of physical activities, but it can provide a rationale for such exploration and choice, and shed some light on the process itself.

The search that culminates in the development of a personal model encompasses a number of aspects of human identity—for example, needs, sexuality, the role of the body—as well as life's meanings and values.

Students can be encouraged to identify their own needs through self-awareness education sessions by reflecting on their experiences and feelings and connecting these needs to physical activities by exploration and choice insofar as the subject matter of physical education and the individual's biological boundaries will permit. If Maslow's need hierarchy, as described by Alderman,[1] is used, the need for safety, belonging, self-esteem, and self-actualization could be met, at least in part, by physical activity. For example, the need for safety and security could be met by selecting safe activities in which to participate, as Alderman suggests, or by developing a repertoire of abilities related to self-protection such as self-defense skills, endurance, speed, and the like, as I have recommended to some students.

The development of sexual identity can be considered a specific need tied directly not only to the body but to sport and exercise in our culture. For example, it has been suggested that sport is the last stronghold of masculinity,[2] and serves as a rite of passage for the American male.[12] As cultural norms widen, both sexes are beginning to explore and to feel more comfortable in activities previously characterized as masculine or feminine. As a result, students are somewhat freer to develop their own concept of sexuality and its relation, if any, to physical activity. Physical education can contribute to this process by helping the student explore the relationship of sexual identity to physical activity and build toward a personal model that affirms his own sexuality.

The whole question of the role of the body in each student's personal model extends the exploration process in physical education even further, and spills over into questions of needs and sexual identity. Each individual must determine the place of physical appearance, physical competence, body awareness, and perhaps kinesthetic satisfaction in his personal model.[9] Certain exploratory experiences are necessary before such determinations can be made, such as experiencing some competence or at least improvement in one or more activities, experiencing some sense of in-creased body awareness as the result of planned body-awareness activities (e.g., relaxation, Feldenkrais, yoga), experiencing the po-tential of specific exercises to change physical appearance, and ex-periencing some kinesthetic satisfaction from moving. These kinds of experiences can sample only some key potentialities of the body, and by inference, widen the base from which to choose attributes that best represent the student's desired identity.

The distinction between a person's search for identity and his search for meaning and values in life is often blurred, but both meanings and values can be identified in a physical education con-text. Physical education activities have traditionally been restricted to a tight cluster of meanings: competitive achievement and its ramifications (e.g., status, self-esteem) and physical health (e.g., the prevention of cardiovascular disease and weight control) head the list. However, as Kenyon's research has shown, there are a number of other meanings that students may find attractive and fulfilling, such as a sense of development from observing one's own im-provement or of strength from a particular performance; social in-teraction as the primary reason for participating; the aesthetic or, more rarely, the ascetic (pain-oriented) aspects of the physical ex-perience; risk taking; the search for peak experiences in sport; the feeling of catharsis—that is, the release of tensions, anxieties, and frustrations.[10] At least some of these meanings can be structured and offered to students to help them build a personal model.

The development of a person's private value system transcends the physical education experience, but physical education as a pro-cess of interaction does provide a setting for exploring and acting in accordance with one's values. Examples of value orientations are love, truth, beauty, integrity, personal power, pleasure, and adven-ture, all of which have relevance for physical education and beyond, and specifically, for building a personal model of behavior. Opportunities for choice in physical education and elsewhere often offer alternatives that can be categorized as helpful, neutral, or detrimental to others and perhaps to one's self as well. Such deci-sions reflect value orientations. Two methods for connecting the valuing process to physical education are values clarification,[19] which stresses the sorting of alternative values and their conse-quences and eventually the choosing and affirming of one's values, and the introduction of values such as love in a physical education context.

Model-building holds little meaning without an implementa-tion stage aimed at changing a student's behavior so that it approximates his personal model. If a student is to be able to modify his own behavior, instruction in techniques of self-control being developed by behaviorists should be included in self-awareness education sessions.[25] Often, humanistically oriented educators, myself included, help students to build a personal model and then leave to faith in humanity the matter of reconciling the student's current behavior with his model. It is one thing to identify a need that physical activity can meet or a value that participation can represent, but it is quite another to convert this insight into practice so that the need is in fact met or the value practiced.

CONCLUSION

I have tried to describe some guidelines for teaching physical education based on a particular goal model and some specific assumptions about man's potentialities. I believe the artistry of the teacher–student relationship is crucial to the student's search for self in a physical education setting, from gaining some sense of personal worth to becoming more aware and more creative and spontaneous. In recognition of the role of intentionality in teaching, I have briefly mentioned a few strategies for meeting the need to feel competent and the creative capacity, and at greater length, I have described a model-building process toward greater self-awareness.

Because I have already mentioned my conviction that man views the world subjectively, it follows that my ideas are subjective, a product of my conscious experience in subjective collaboration with observations and the research and ideas of others. Yet somehow they come out as truth, or as Bridges put it, humanists tend toward "a kind of specious personalism, which is the object-oriented world view recast in the first person."[2] I can only add, rather feebly, that the thoughts expressed here are not intended to be "etched in stone"—they are more process than product. The only certainty is that these ideas, like others before them, will be clarified, revised, and even (horrors) discarded in my continuing search for self in physical education and in life. Feel free to do the same.

REFERENCES

1. Alderman, R. B.: *Psychological Behavior in Sport.* Philadelphia: W. B. Saunders Co., 1974.
2. Beisser, A. R.: *The Madness in Sport.* New York: Appleton-Century-Crofts, 1967.

3. Bridges, B.: *Teachers Can Make a Difference* by Gerald F. Corey. *AHP Newsletter*, June, 1974, pp. 10–11.
4. Cohen, S., and Hersch, R.: Behaviorism and humanism: A synthesis for teacher education. *Journal of Teacher Education, XXIII:* 172–176, 1972.
5. Combs, A. W.: Some basic concepts for teacher education. *Journal of Teacher Education, XXIII:* 286–290, 1974.
6. Combs, A. W., and Snygg, D.: *Individual Behavior: A Perceptual Approach to Behavior*, rev. ed. New York: Harper & Row, Publishers, 1959.
7. Drews, E., and Lipson, L.: *Values and Humanity*. New York: St. Martin's Press, 1971.
7a. Fait, H. F., and Billing, J. E.: Reassessment of the value of competition. In *Issues in Physical Education and Sport*. Edited by G. H. McGlynn. San Francisco: National Press Books, 1974, pp. 15–22.
8. Gerber, E. W.: *Innovators and Institutions in Physical Education*. Philadelphia: Lea & Febiger, 1971.
9. Harris, D. V.: *Involvement in Sport: A Somatopsychic Rationale for Physical Activity*. Philadelphia: Lea & Febiger, 1973.
10. Kenyon, G. S.: *Values Held for Physical Activity by Selected Urban Secondary School Students in Canada, Australia, England and the Unites States*. Madison, Wis.: University of Wisconsin Press, 1968.
11. Locke, L. F.: Physical Education: If I Had It My Way. Paper presented at National AAHPER Convention, Minneapolis, March, 1973.
12. Malina, R. M.: An anthropological perspective of man in action. In *New Perspectives of Man in Action*. Edited by R. C. Brown and B. J. Cratty. Englewood Cliffs, N.J.: Prentice-Hall, Inc., 1969, pp. 147–162.
13. Mosston, M., and Mueller, R.: Mission, Omission, and Submission in Physical Education. *Proceedings of the National Physical Education Association for Men, LXXIII:* 122–130, 1969.
14. Oden, T. C.: A populist's view of psychotherapeutic deprofessionalization. *Journal of Humanistic Psychology, XIV:* 3–18, 1974.
15. Patterson, C. H.: *Humanistic Education*. Englewood Cliffs, N.J.: Prentice-Hall, Inc., 1973.
16. Polanyi, M.: *Personal Knowledge*. Chicago: University of Chicago Press, 1958.
17. Polanyi, M.: *Science, Faith, and Society*. Chicago: University of Chicago Press, 1964.
18. Powell, J.: *Why Am I Afraid to Tell You Who I Am?* Niles, Ill.: Argus Communications, 1969.
19. Raths, L.E., et al.: *Values and Teaching*. Columbus, Ohio: Charles E. Merrill Publishing Company, 1966.
20. Siedentop, D.: *Physical Education: Introductory Analysis*. Dubuque: William C. Brown Company, Publishers, 1972a.
21. Siedentop, D.: Behavior analysis and teacher training. *Quest, XVIII:* 26–32, 1972b.
22. Singer, R. N., and Dick, W.: *Teaching Physical Education: A Systems Approach*. Boston: The Houghton Mifflin Company, 1974.
23. Smith, M. B.: On self-actualization: A transambivalent examination of a focal theme in Maslow's psychology. *Journal of Humanistic Psychology, XIII:* 17–33, 1973.
24. The Simple Solutions. *Manas, XXVII:* 1 ff, 1974.
25. Thoresen, C. E.: Behavioral Humanism. In *Behavior Modification in Education*. 1973 NSEE Yearbook, I. Chicago: University of Chicago Press, 1973, pp. 385–421.

Chapter 5

A Behavioral Perspective for Humanistic Objectives

Frank Rife

Educators can and should act to help individuals experience life in more positive ways. This task has been undertaken by various groups of individuals in education, primarily those who label themselves humanists, and more recently, by groups of individuals labeling themselves behaviorists or behavioral scientists. Several procedures encouraging this positive experience have been suggested,[8,12,13,34] and one method offers considerable promise. This method is a synthesis of the principles and techniques of social-learning and behaviorism with the concerns and goals of humanistic education. The work of both the humanist and the behaviorist can be aided if we alleviate some of the confusion and ambiguities concerning contemporary humanism and behaviorism, and utilize newer scientific methods geared to the study of human phenomena. Distinctions between humanists and behaviorists do exist, but the issue is not really humanism versus behaviorism but focuses on other issues. The concern of this chapter will be how best to utilize the concepts and methodologies of both areas to help others and to help oneself develop better self-control.

Many people have written about the concern of humanistic education and psychology.[1,5,8,13,22] Discussions have had a wide range of approaches and directions, and this is at once a strength and a weakness. The exclusion of boundaries ensures that nothing is left out, yet the lack of a coherent, defined, integrated, and theoretical rationale in humanistic psychology has hindered empirical research in the field. Fantini has mentioned that the humanist must be "one who does."[9] Buhler has suggested that the goals of humanism can be attained if scientific methods are used to help the individual experience his existence as real.[5] This means that the humanist must be more action-oriented as opposed to the traditional view of one engaged in philosophical disputes and arguments.

The behaviorist also suffers in the contemporary eye because he has been accused of implying that a human being is not unique and dynamic, but only a bundle of reflexes and movements that cannot escape environmental control. Much of this viewpoint can be traced to the early behavioral work of the American psychologist John B. Watson and of the Russian physiologist Ivan Pavlov. Both men made careful observation of animal behavior and then inferred that human behavior had no distinguishing characteristics. This was dangerous at a time when so little was really known about behavior, particularly human behavior. But the puppet-on-the-string image has changed, along with the behaviorist's position.

Several humanistic psychologists believe the key to good behavior is the "positive experience," and suggest creating environments that nurture this positive atmosphere. This, in turn, directs the individual toward greater self-actualization.[5,8,16,22,23] It is curious that this humanistic position of the importance of the positive environment approaches the stand of many contemporary behavioral therapists, counselors, and operant psychologists who also consider themselves humanists.[14,15,21,33] Results of behavioral research also encourage the use of situations in which a person can "experience" positive feedback from his or her behavior. Positive feedback increases the *probability* of that behavior's recurring. The more a person can "manage" his environment in order to emit successful behaviors, the more he has increased his awareness and potential for attaining a fuller self-actualization. Perhaps the focused efforts of these behaviorists can clarify some similarities of these two positions. First, the individual's behavior is viewed as being learned through interaction with the environment, that is, the self is learned rather than given. Second, because the environment is construed as contributing to possible problems in human behavior, it is analyzed and altered with the intention of reducing and preventing such problems.[19] Third, the behaviorist also focuses on a person's behavior, what he actually *does*, and not who he is in terms of ambiguous social terms and labels. Finally, behaviorists use developed methods to improve techniques for helping human beings. This last characteristic is also mentioned as one of the concerns of humanistic psychology.[37] Research techniques that provide intensive study into human behavioral phenomena and avoid the detachment and impersonality of the traditional methods of physical science are also advocated by many contemporary behaviorists.[18,26,32,36,42]

Traditional research designs and techniques are inadequate for the necessary intimate and intensive study of the individual. They have relied on large groups of subjects and elaborate statistical techniques that indicate a mean performance for that group. These designs are concerned with one facet of the cycle of scientific inquiry, that of observing, defining, testing, induction, deduction, discovery, and verification.[18,26]

Fortunately, an alternate design of great promise has been developed, one that has had a long and honorable history in science,[6,7,25,27,29] and that has been applied with success in many different situations.[3,4,6,10,11,12,24,35,39,41] This design is referred to as the N =1 experimental design, and is based on the behavioral model of operant psychology. The operant model focuses on the relationship between the behavior or response of an individual and the *consequences* of that response. This relationship is referred to as a *contingency* and the consequences serve as feedback for the individual. The following diagrams illustrate the four basic contingencies of operant psychology: (S) refers to a stimulus situation; (S^D) refers to a discriminative stimulus situation; (R) refers to the response of the individual; (Re) refers to reinforcement; and P(r) refers to probability of response.

1. (S)→(R)→(Re +): P(r) ↑

A response is positively reinforced by a previously undefined situation, and the probability of this response recurring is increased.

2. (S)→(R)→(Re −): P(r) ↓

A response is negatively reinforced by a previously undefined situation, and the probability of this response recurring is decreased.

3. (S^D)→(R)→(Re +): P(r:D^S) ↑

A response is positively reinforced by a discriminative stimulus, and the probability of this response recurring is increased in the presence of this discriminative stimulus.

4. (S^D)→(R)→(Re −): P(r:D^S) ↓

A response is negatively reinforced by a discriminative stimulus, and the probability of this response recurring is decreased in the presence of this discriminative stimulus.

The last two examples are diagrams of situations in which the individual has had previous experience. Thus, the last two paradigms demonstrate the dual function of discriminative stimuli, being (1) a cue for increasing or decreasing the probability of a behavior, and (2) a function of reinforcement. This makes the learning paradigm

$$(R) \rightarrow \left[\begin{array}{c} S^D \\ Re \pm \end{array} \right] : P(r),$$

the brackets indicating the double function. The reinforcements associated with the situational stimuli combine to increase or decrease the probability of similar behaviors recurring when the individual again finds himself in a similar situation. For example, if an individual has experienced the opportunity of helping someone and received a smile or a "thank you" (Re +) in return, the next time he sees a similar opportunity (S^D) the likelihood of his offering his help again (R) is increased because of the "thanks" (Re +) he received in the similar circumstance (S^D). A "thank you," a smile, or signs of concern form one of the strongest types of reinforcement in our society, that of social reinforcers.[2,40]

The teacher is in an obvious position to take advantage of this important aspect of reinforcement feedback for an individual's behavior. But how does he accomplish this? How will he know if his encouragement and reinforcement is having any effect? The N =1 design offers such a tool.

The first step in using such a technique is to know what behavior or goal of behavior the teacher is going to observe in his students. The teacher must know what it is he will be looking for before he can ever hope to encourage that behavior in his students. He must have an operable definition, stated in such a way as to be observable and measurable. This defined goal is referred to as the *target behavior*. The *crucial* aspect is that the desired behavioral goal be defined accurately. Measurement is not a problem, for science has provided us with instruments that can measure even the smallest instances of human behavior, once an operable definition has been obtained. But this should not worry the teacher, as most classroom behavior is not of the molecular type but of the molar type. For example, if a teacher wants to increase the interpersonal relations of a particular student, he must have an operable definition of interpersonal relations in observable and measurable terms. The definition may be very situational for any specific teacher. In a gymnastics class, the goal of interpersonal relations might be defined as the number of times a student helps others perform a particular gymnastic stunt. Increasing interpersonal relations may be construed as spotting, holding someone's legs, or helping a classmate onto a high bar. The desirable increase may be any number the teacher deems necessary.

Once the teacher has formulated a workable definition for observation purposes, he must ensure that the defined goal is free of any observer bias, in this case, his own. This necessitates another observer to aid in the observing and recording of the behavior in question. This person can be a team-teaching partner, a teacher's aide, or possibly a student–teacher. The best way to eliminate possible bias is to have both teacher and observer practice the use of the developed definition until they arrive at a level of agreement of at least 80 per cent. This is referred to as attaining *interobserver reliability*. Interobserver agreement is calculated as

$$\frac{\text{Agreements}}{\text{Agreements} + \text{Disagreements}} \times 100 = \% \text{ of Agreement.}$$

Once this level of agreement is reached, the teacher is ready to make observations. A starting point must be made to determine if the student under observation already emits any of the target behaviors. This determination is referred to as establishing a *baseline*. This can be done in several ways. During a five-minute period of a class, the teacher may watch the student to see how many times he performs the defined behavior. Recording each instance of behavior during the five-minute period is termed *event recording*. The teacher may observe several five-minute segments during a single class period, or may observe only one five-minute segment during each class period. The teacher can plot the number of behaviors on a graph such as that shown in Figure 5–1. The teacher should observe for five or six five-minute periods before initiating any type of *intervention* of reinforcement feedback on the student under observation. *Intervention should not be made on the initial baseline behaviors unless the plot of behaviors is shown to be either stable or continuing in a manner opposite the desired outcome.* At least once during this baseline period the teacher should conduct a reliability of interobserver agreement.

Intervention can come in the form of reinforcement feedback to the student after each instance of his behavior in question. The teacher can begin this intervention by praising each instance of student behavior defined as leading to interpersonal relations. The same observation-recording techniques are used as were used in

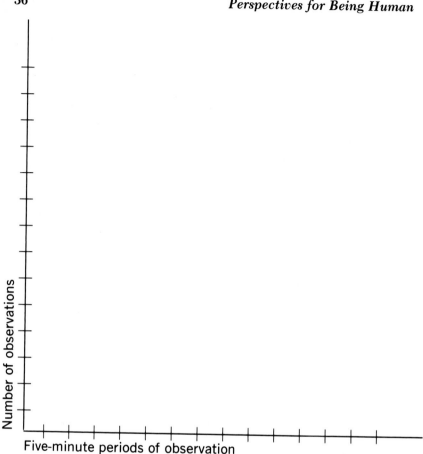

Figure 5–1. Graph for plotting behavior to establish a baseline.

the initial baseline procedures. The difference now is that the teacher will not only record each instance of behavior but also praise it. Social reinforcers have been shown to be effective in increasing certain behaviors,[2,40] and in this instance, would encourage the student to increase his cooperative behavior and sensitivity toward others.

An important aspect of this design for making a behavioral change is that the student must not become dependent on being reinforced by the teacher for each act of cooperation. The natural reinforcing consequences of the particular situation must begin to replace the reinforcement feedback of the teacher, but this is not as great a problem as it may appear. The effect of the teacher as a model has been shown to be important in behavioral change,[17,25,27] and students will imitate teacher behavior with or without the teacher's intention. If students realize they can receive the teacher's praise and attention for exhibiting cooperative behavior, they may exhibit more of it. This natural reinforcement in the social situation of the classroom allows the teacher to gradually reduce his praising of the individual student and let the classroom students perform this function.

The techniques of the operant model have also been encouraged for the attainment of greater self-control. A behavioral approach views self-control as a complex interaction of internal and external responses. It views the ability to manage or control oneself as a valued human act, a learned phenomenon, and therefore that everyone is capable of attaining it. This also implies that everyone is then responsible and accountable for his actions.

Giving the person the power to change is the central focus of this procedure, encouraging what some existential-phenomenologists have termed a "personal scientist."[16] By the observation and recording of personal behaviors, the individual presents himself with a picture of the frequencies of his behavior and the environments associated with encouraging these behaviors.

Self-control is not viewed as a distinct category of behavior detached from external control or other methods of behavioral influence. It is conceptualized as a continuum in which internal and external control interact to influence behavior.[20] An angry husband or an overweight individual may use different self-control techniques to act more positively toward his wife or to reduce his eating habits, but either individual will also be influenced by external factors such as reactions from other members of his family or concerns for his health.

A fuller understanding of self-control necessitates a distinction between self-controlled (RC) and self-controlling responses (SCR).[37] Self-controlling responses are used to influence the desired responses to be controlled yet both are subject to environmental influences. For example, during a basketball game, a player at the free-throw line may practice self-controlling behaviors (SCR) of relaxation and mental rehearsal of the components of a good shot in order to increase the probability of making a free throw, a response he wishes to control (RC).

A practical and real problem for a person trying to change his own actions is how to maintain his self-controlling behaviors (SCR). These behaviors are influenced by the external environment (e.g., a game situation, social comments), and a major task for the individual is to arrange his environment to aid rather than to discourage his self-controlling behaviors. For example, it would prove difficult for a person to reduce his smoking behavior if he is continually in the company of other smokers who offer him a cigarette. It therefore makes sense to consider self-control as a continuum of various activities rather than as a category or an entity opposed to external control.

Self-controlling responses (SCR) may be exercised through several strategies, with self-observation and environmental planning having great merit and application. These two methodologies are not exclusive of one another, as one procedure can certainly incorporate items from the other. The results of self-observation may require an individual to remove himself from or to change his environment in order to encourage or discourage certain behaviors.

In order to observe and record a behavior to be controlled (RC), a person must be aware of the behavior. Self-observation techniques present one way to develop this needed awareness. The person first gathers data on the behavior he wishes to change (RC) *before* he initiates any intervention technique. The problem, and yet the power, of self-observation as a technique for change relies on a *systematic* and *consistent* method of observation and recording. Such a process provides the individual with an ongoing system of feedback, a system that will invariably influence the behavior under observation. The person who systematically observes and records his behavior is increasing his capability of self-awareness. This increased self-awareness can contribute to a fuller self-actualization.

Wall charts, wrist-counters, and behavioral diaries are a few of the techniques of self-observation, a few of the many that need closer scrutiny. A wall chart of weight in the bathroom or a wrist-counter for recording positive self-thoughts can reflect trends and changes, such as weekend responses compared to weekday responses. This tally would provide feedback on gradual changes that might otherwise go unnoticed. Self-recorded data can also present important information on such items as the rate of a behavior, what environments tend to elicit this behavior, and what consequences may be maintaining it. In essence, recording devices provide an objective basis for self-evaluation. If the information gathered indicates that the individual is changing in a desired direction, then he has an excellent basis for having positive feelings about himself. If the person has not moved in a desired direction, he has a more secure base from which to initiate an intervention for change.

A second self-controlling strategy involves altering one's

environment so either the discriminative stimulus cues (S^D), which precede the behavior, or the behavior's immediate consequences are changed. This alteration of the environment may involve a reduction in, or an avoidance of, daily situations for which a decision has to be made. The overweight individual may discover much of his between-meal eating is concurrent with watching television. The gradual reduction of time spent watching television, say only after 9:00 P.M., represents a restricted stimulus situation and can reduce the concomitant response of eating. The physical environment such as the kitchen or den may also elicit excessive eating responses. Having a meal in another room without all the discriminative cues to eat can also reduce the amount eaten.

Upper and Meredith altered the smoking habits of long-standing heavy smokers by changing the physical cues to smoke.[38] Smokers recorded their daily smoking rate, and set the buzzer on small portable timers for their average intercigarette interval. They then smoked only *after* the timer buzzed. By establishing this new cue to smoke, previous discriminative cues for smoking such as a cup of coffee, completing a meal, or talking with a friend were reduced or eliminated. The establishment of new cues was done completely under the individual's control and helped him reduce his undesirable smoking behavior.

In addition to the alteration of discriminative stimuli, a second type of environmental programming involves altering the external *consequences* of a behavior. In some instances, the natural consequences of the environment may provide this function. Many drug users suffer from an unrewarding use of a drug and discontinue their drug-using behavior. The individual, however, may not want to rely on the intermittent schedule of positive or negative consequences provided by the natural environment, and makes arrangements to have a wife or close friend provide certain positive or negative consequences when his RC occurs. After smoking a cigarette, a husband might ask his wife to remind him of his doctor's advice to reduce his smoking or mention the possible contribution of smoking to lung cancer. A husband might also ask his wife to praise him or make a favorite dessert after abstaining from smoking over a certain period of time.

Contingency-based point systems or tokens are other examples of environmental planning for self-control. A person can arrange to receive a certain number of points or tokens (money) contingent on the occurrence or nonoccurrence of a behavior. Being rewarded for work done is like the piecemeal pay schedule of a factory. The more a person is rewarded for doing things that help him, the greater the likelihood he will continue the self-helping behaviors and increase his personal worth and self-esteem. Such planning allows the individual to take advantage of the powerful effects of his environment and to increase his personal meaning and satisfaction.

Humanistic psychologists and educators share much in common with contemporary behaviorists. All are concerned with increasing the understanding of human behavior. The behavioral approach is simple and *may* fail to capture all human phenomena. But moving from the simple to the complex has been one of the most successful procedures of modern science.[23] In an area where little empirical information has been generated, it is crucial to have empirically derived data in order to move from the simplistic position.[28] A major problem concerns a methodology that will encourage more humanistic behavior. If a methodology is too simple, then indeed it will not work. The answer is to be found empirically, not by an argumentative process. With such information we can increase our knowledge and help the individual engage in more self-actualizing behavior.

REFERENCES

1. Allport, G.: *Personality: A Psychological Interpretation.* New York: Holt, Rinehart, and Winston, 1937.
2. Ayllon, T., and Michael, J.: The psychiatric nurse as a behavioral engineer. J. Exp. Anal. Behav., 2:323–334, 1959.
3. Baer, D. M., Wolf, M. M., and Risley, T. R.: Some current dimensions of applied behavior analysis. J. Appl. Behav. Anal., *1*:91–97, 1968.
4. Browning, R. M., and Stover, D. D.: *Behavior Modification in Child Treatment.* Chicago: Aldine-Atherton, 1971.
5. Buhler, C.: Basic theoretical concepts of humanistic psychology. *Am. Psychol.,* 26:378–386, 1971.
6. Cooper, J. O.: *Measurement and Analysis of Behavioral Techniques.* Columbus, Ohio: Charles E. Merrill Publishing Co., 1974.
7. Dukes, W. F.: N =1. *Psychol. Bull.,* 64:74–79, 1965.
8. Fantini, M., and Weinstein, G., (Eds.): *Toward Humanistic Education: A Curriculum of Affect.* New York: Praeger Publishers, Inc., 1970.
9. Fantini, M.: Humanizing the humanism movement. *The Phi Delta Kappan,* pp. 400–402, February, 1974.
10. Graubard, P. S., Rosenburg, H., and Miller, M.: Student applications of behavior modification to teachers and environments or ecological approaches to social deviancy, 1, 2. In *A New Direction for Education: Behavior Analysis 1971.* Edited by E. A. Ramp and B. L. Hopkins. Lawrence, Kan.: The University of Kansas, Department of Human Development, 1971, pp. 80–100.
11. Hall, R. V.: *Behavior Modification: The Measurement of Behavior.* Lawrence, Kan.: H and H Enterprises, Inc., 1971.
12. Hall, R. V.: *Behavior Modification: Applications in School and Home.* Lawrence, Kan.: H and H Enterprises, Inc., 1971.

13. Hellison, D. R.: *Humanistic Physical Education.* Englewood Cliffs, N.J.: Prentice-Hall, Inc., 1973.
14. Hosford, R. E., and Zimmer, J.: Humanism through behaviorism. *Counseling and Values,* 16:1–7, 1972.
15. Kanfer, F. H., and Phillips, J. S.: *Learning Foundations of Behavior Therapy.* New York: John Wiley & Sons, 1970.
16. Kelly, G.: *The Psychology of Personal Constructs,* Vol. 1, New York: W. W. Norton & Co., 1955.
17. Koran, J. J.: The Relative Effects of Imitation Versus Problem Solving on the Acquisition of Inquiry Behavior by Intern Teachers. Stanford, Calif.: Stanford University, Stanford Center for Research and Development in Teaching, May, 1970.
18. Lackenmeyer, C. W.: Experimentation—A misunderstood methodology in psychological and social-psychological research. *Am. Psychol.,* 25:617–624, 1970.
19. Lewin, K.: *A Dynamic Theory of Personality-Selected Papers.* New York: McGraw-Hill Book Co., 1935.
20. London, P.: *Behavior Control.* New York: Harper & Row, 1969.
21. MacCorquodale, K.: Behavorism is a humanism. *Humanist,* 31:12–13, 1971.
22. Maslow, A. H.: Towards a humanistic biology. *Am. Psychol.,* 24:724–735, 1965.
23. Maslow, A. H.: *The Psychology of Science.* New York: Harper & Row, 1966.
24. Millenson, J. R.: *Principles of Behavioral Analysis.* New York: The Macmillan Company, 1967.
25. Orme, M. E., and Oliver, W. F.: The Effects of Modeling and Feedback Variables on the Acquisition of a Complex Teaching Strategy. Unpublished doctoral dissertation. Stanford, Calif.: Stanford University, 1966.
26. Paul, G. L.: Behavior modification research: Design and tactics. In *Behavior Therapy: Appraisal and Status.* Edited by C. Frank. New York: McGraw-Hill Book Co., 1969, pp. 29–62.
27. Rife, F.: The Modifications of Student-Teacher Behavior and its Effects Upon Pupil-Behavior. Unpublished doctoral dissertation. Columbus, Ohio: The Ohio State University, 1973.
28. Risley, T. R.: Behavior Modification: An Experimental-Therapeutic Endeavor. Unpublished paper prepared for the Banff International Conference on Behavior Modification, April, 1969.
29. Sidman, M.: *The Tactics of Scientific Research: Evaluating Experimental Data in Psychology.* New York: Basic Books, 1960.
30. Reference deleted.
31. Reference deleted.
32. Skinner, B. F.: A case history in scientific method. In *Psychology: A Study of Science,* Vol. 2. Edited by S. Koch. New York: McGraw-Hill Book Co., 1959.
33. Skinner, B. F.: *Beyond Freedom and Dignity.* New York: Alfred Knopf, 1971.
34. Skinner, B. F.: *About Behaviorism.* New York: Alfred Knopf, 1974.
35. Smith, W., and Moore, J. W.: *Conditioning and Instrumental Learning.* New York: McGraw-Hill Book Co., 1966.
36. Thoresen, Carl E.: Relevance and research in counseling. *Rev. Educ. Res.,* 39:264–282, 1969.
37. Thoresen, Carl E.: Behavioral humanism. In *Behavior Modification in Education.* Edited by C. E. Thoresen. Chicago: The University of Chicago Press, 1973.
38. Upper, D., and Meredith, L.: A Stimulus Control Approach to the Modification of Smoking Behavior. *Proceedings of the 78th Annual Convention,* American Psychological Association, 1970.
39. Williams, R. L., and Anandam, K.: *Cooperative Classroom Management.* Columbus, Ohio: Charles E. Merrill Publishing Co., 1973.

40. Wolf, M. M., Risley, T., and Mees, H.: Application of operant conditioning procedures to the behavior problems of an autistic child. *Behav. Res. Ther.,* 1:305–312, 1964.
41. Wolf, M., and Risley, T.: Reinforcement: Applied research. In *The Nature of Reinforcement.* Edited by R. Glaser. New York: Academic Press, 1971, pp. 310–325.
42. Yates, A.: *Behavior Therapy.* New York: John Wiley & Sons, 1970.

GENERAL READING

Siedentop, D.: The humanistic education movement: Some questions. In *Issues in Physical Education and Sport.* Edited by G. McGlynn. Palo Alto, Calif.: National Press Books, 1974.

SECTION II

INCREASING LEVELS OF CONSCIOUSNESS

Chapter 6

Introduction

Cosmic consciousness, transcendental unconscious, peak experience, enlightenment, illumination, and liberation are all somewhat suggestive of states of awareness that are unique from our normal, everyday waking consciousness.

The authors of chapters in this section intimate that such perceptions can have a transforming effect on the person who experiences them. To the unknowing observer there are perhaps no outward behavioral signs that something unique is happening. But to one engaged in such experiential processes, an inner mystery reveals itself, sometimes dramatically.

With only casual observation I think one might be justified in suggesting that there is a basic drive in living matter to extend itself, and in the process to become more, to be better, to transcend self. Personally meaningful involvement in various forms of physical activity may indeed be the path, and perhaps the light, to a more fully functioning integrated existence for the person who chooses such an extension. As professionals, perhaps one of our greatest responsibilities may be to expose the *way* to others and to share the skills necessary for others to travel the path in an atmosphere of comfort, security, and encouragement.

It would seem that for such processes to take place, we also need to be more open to some of the less recognized dimensions of our discipline which we have previously disregarded. We must be careful not to automatically screen out those sensory data that we have been culturally conditioned to disallow. The input of such data may have potentially enlightening consequences. Therefore, we need to adopt a position suggesting that all moments are real, potent, significant, and meaningful for the person who experiences them. In doing so, we make ourselves more aware that we are aware.

As I read the chapters, many of the authors may be describing, whether or not knowingly, a unique form of enlightenment which may greatly assist in human revelation and perhaps personal evolution. Continuously the call must be for all of us to experience these states directly. If we allow the past conditioning of our minds to filter these unique perceptions of consciousness, an immediate hindrance will be placed on our level of understanding, thereby reducing the potential significance of such experiences.

Each of the writers continuously calls for a focus on the uniqueness of the individual as he or she experiences physical activity, with an emphasis on the potential *meaning* that such experiences have for the person. In addition, a strong emotional character in these experiences, in which the depictions are similar to and consistent with other writings in this book, seems to call for humankind to return to sensual-emotive bases.

On reading Charles Tart's chapter, one is led to ask if there is a possibility for out-of-the-body experiences (OOBEs) to occur in sport movement-related environments. The interrelatedness and dependence of an OOBE on an alive, fully functioning body suggest to some extent that sport movement situations are indeed potentially ripe for the occurrence of such experiences. It would seem that certain mental states experienced in sport do have similarities to certain accounts of parapsychological phenomena.

There also seem to be some similarities between Tart's OOBEs and Ken Ravizza's depiction of peak-experiences in sport. Of course, many of the peak-experience characteristics are different from those suggested for OOBEs, so I do not imply that the two are the same, merely that selected characteristics of each are similar.

First, OOBEs and peak-experiences are difficult to describe, perhaps primarily owing to the limitations of language. Such limitation should not be an excuse to diminish the integrity and potential worthwhileness of both experiences. Second, both have been described as being sometimes intense and scary, sometimes joyous, but always memorable moments for the person who experiences them.

Carolyn Thomas particularizes her descriptions to the realm of aesthetics in sport and movement events as seen from the performer's perspective. Here again, one is cautioned to consider the experiences not synonymously but only similarly, and to treat them as having the potential to expand our view of reality in general and our perspective of human experiences in sport and movement more specifically. She contends that physical activity is indeed a meaningful form, which allows one to seek and perhaps find some of what is beautiful about human existence.

Peggy Gazette and Margaret Hukill call for us to recognize the potentially spiritual quality of human involvement during certain movement events. They suggest that some activities present the possibility for human beings to experience oneness and a certain sense of self that transcend traditional categories of understanding.

On reading this section, a number of possible conclusions appear. First, it would seem that we, of all professionals, should be masters of the moving center! Is this not the essence of our profession—teaching individuals to move as integrated, unified beings? Second, it seems that our current view of reality is somewhat restrictive, thereby reducing phenomena that do not fit into already existing categories to an inconsequential status. Third, the human self does indeed extend beyond the border of its own organism; we are connected to other beings and our environment in ways that science has yet to comprehend. Last, as suggested earlier, if we are indeed concerned with a truly comprehensive understanding of human beings involved in movement, we must feel confident in drawing ideas from a number of professional disciplines and philosophical positions which we have previously disregarded or misunderstood.

Chapter 7

Introduction from Monroe's Journeys Out of the Body*

Charles T. Tart

In our action-oriented society, when a man lies down to sleep, he is effectively out of the picture. He will lie still for six to eight hours, so he is not "behaving," "thinking productively," or doing anything "significant." We all know that people dream, but we raise our children to regard dreams and other experiences occurring during sleep as unimportant, as not *real* in the way that the events of the day are. Thus most people are in the habit of forgetting their dreams, and, on the occasions when they do remember them, they usually regard them as mere oddities.

It is true that psychologists and psychiatrists regard the dreams of patients as useful clues to the malfunctioning of their personalities; but even in this application dreams and other nocturnal experiences are generally not treated as *real* in any sense, but only as some sort of internal data processing of the human computer.

There are some important exceptions to this general put-down of dreams, but for the vast majority of people in our society today, dreams are not things that serious people concern themselves with.

What are we to make of a person who takes exception to this general belief, who claims to have had experiences during sleep or other forms of unconsciousness that were not only *impressive* to him, but which he feels were *real?*

Suppose this person claims that on the previous night he had an experience of flying through the air over a large city which he soon recognized as New York. Further, he tells us that not only was this "dream" intensely vivid, but that he knew *at the time* that it was not a dream, that he was really in the air over New York City. And this conviction that he was *really* there sticks with him for the rest of his life, despite our reminding him that a sleeping man couldn't really be flying by himself in the air over New York City.

*Introduction from *Journeys Out of the Body* by Robert A. Monroe. Copyright © 1971 by Robert A. Monroe. Reprinted by permission of Doubleday & Company, Inc.

Probably we will ignore a person who makes such a report, or we will politely (or not so politely) inform him that he is becoming a little weak in the head or crazy, and suggest that he see a psychotherapist. If he is insistent about the reality of his experience, especially if he has other strange experiences too, we may with the best of intentions see about committing him to a mental hospital.

Our "traveler," on the other hand, if he is smart, will quickly learn not to talk about his experiences. The only problem with that, as I have found from talking to many such people, is that he may worry about whether he's going crazy.

For the sake of argument, let's make our "traveler" even more troubling. Suppose in his account he goes on to say that after flying over New York City for a while he flew down to your apartment. There he saw you and two other people, unknown to him, conversing. He describes the two people in detail, and mentions a few things about the topic of conversation occurring in the minute or so he was there.

Let's suppose he is correct. At the time he had his experience, you were holding a conversation on the topic he mentions with two people who fit our "traveler's" descriptions. What do we make of things now?

The usual reaction to a hypothetical situation of this type is that it is all very interesting, but as we know that it couldn't possibly happen, we needn't seriously think about what it might mean. Or we might comfort ourselves by invoking the word "coincidence." A marvelous word, "coincidence," for relieving mental upsets!

Unfortunately for our peace of mind, there are thousands of instances, reported by normal people, of exactly this sort of occurrence. We are not dealing with a purely hypothetical situation.

Such events have been termed traveling clairvoyance, astral projection, or, a more scientific term, out-of-the-body experiences (OOBEs). We can formally define an OOBE as an event in which the experiencer (1) seems to perceive some portion of some environment which could not possibly be perceived from where his physical body is known to be at the time; and (2) knows *at the time* that he is not dreaming or fantasizing. The experiencer seems to possess his normal consciousness at the time, and even though he may reason that this cannot be happening, he will feel all his normal critical faculties to be present, and so knows he is not dreaming. Further, he will not decide after awakening that this was a dream. How, then, do we understand this strange phenomenon?

If we look to scientific sources for information about OOBEs, we shall find practically none at all. Scientists have, by and large, simply not paid any attention to these phenomena. The situation is rather similar to that of the scientific literature on extrasensory perception (ESP). Phenomena such as telepathy, clairvoyance, precognition, and psychokinesis are "impossible" in terms of the current physical world view. Since they can't happen, most scientists do not bother to read the evidence indicating that they do happen; hence, not having read the evidence, their belief in the impossibility of such phenomena is reinforced. This kind of circular reasoning in support of one's comfortable belief system is not unique to scientists by any means, but it has resulted in very little scientific research on ESP or OOBEs.

In spite of the lack of "hard" scientific data, there are still a number of definite conclusions one can make from reading what material there is.

First, OOBEs are a universal human experience, not in the sense that they happen to large numbers of people, but in that they have happened all through recorded history, and there are marked similarities in the experience among people who are otherwise extremely different in terms of cultural background. One can find reports of OOBEs by housewives in Kansas which closely resemble accounts of OOBEs from ancient Egyptian or oriental sources.

Second, the OOBE is generally a once-in-a-lifetime experience, seemingly experienced by "accident." Illnesses sometimes bring it about, especially illnesses which are almost fatal. Great emotional stress sometimes brings it about. In many cases, it simply happens during sleep without our having any idea of what might have caused it. In very rare instances it seems to have been brought about by a deliberate attempt.

Third, the experience of an OOBE is usually one of the most profound experiences of a person's life, and radically alters his beliefs. This is usually expressed as, "I no longer *believe* in survival of death or an immortal soul, I *know* that I will survive death." The person feels that he has directly experienced being alive and conscious without his physical body, and therefore knows that he possesses some kind of soul that will survive bodily death. This does not logically follow, for even if the OOBE is more than just an interesting dream or hallucination, it was still occurring while the physical body was alive and functioning and therefore may depend on the physical body. This argument, however, makes no impression on those who have actually had an OOBE. Thus regardless of what position one wants to take on the "reality" of the OOBE, it is clearly an experience deserving considerable psychological study. I am certain that our ideas concerning the existence of souls have resulted from early experiences of people having OOBEs. Considering the importance of the idea of the soul to most of our religions, and the importance of religion in people's lives, it seems incredible that science could have swept this problem under the rug so easily.

Fourth, the OOBE is generally extremely joyful to those who have it. I would make a rough estimate that between 90 and 95 per cent of the people who have this experience are very glad it occurred and find it joyful, while 5 per cent are very frightened by it, for the only way they can interpret it, while it is happening, is that they are dying. Later reactions of the person as he attempts to interpret his OOBE can be rather negative, however. Almost every time I give a speech on this subject, someone comes up to me afterward and thanks me for talking about it. They had had the experience some time before, but had no way of explaining it, and worried that they were going "crazy."

Fifth, in some instances of OOBEs the description of what was happening at a distant place is correct and more accurate than we would expect by coincidence. Not the majority, by any means, but some. To explain these we must postulate either that the "hallucinatory" experience of the OOBE was combined with the operation of ESP, or that in some sense the person really was "there." The OOBE then becomes very real indeed.

The fact that most of our knowledge about OOBEs comes from reports of once-in-a-lifetime experiences puts us at two serious disadvantages. The first of these is that most people cannot produce an OOBE at will, so this precludes the possibility of studying them under precise laboratory conditions. The second disadvantage is that when a person is suddenly thrust for a brief period of time into a very novel environment he may not be a very good observer. He is too excited and too busy trying to cope with the strangeness of it. Thus our reports from the once-in-a-lifetime people are very rough. It would be of great advantage in studying OOBEs to have trained "travelers" available who could produce the experience at will and who generally had the characteristics of a good reporter.

When most people have a profound experience, especially one with religious import, careful questioning will usually reveal that their original account of it was not so much an account of what happened as of what they thought it meant. As an example, let us suppose that what really happens to a person is that he finds himself floating in the air above his body, in the middle of the night; while still surprised at this, he perceives a shadowy, dim figure at the end of the room, and then a blue circle of light floats past the figure from left to right. Then our experiencer loses consciousness and wakes up to find himself in his body. A good reporter will describe essentially that scene. Many people will say, in perfectly good faith, something like, "My immortal soul was raised from the tomb of my body by the grace of God last night, and an angel appeared. As a symbol of God's favor, the angel showed me a symbol of wholeness."

I have often seen distortions this great when I've been able to question an individual about exactly what happened, but most of the published accounts of OOBEs have not been subjected to this kind of questioning. The statements that God's will caused the OOBE, that the dim figure turned into an angel, that the blue circle was a symbol of wholeness are all things that are part of a person's *interpretation,* not his *experience.* Most people are not aware of the extent to which their mind automatically interprets things. They think they are perceiving things as they are.

Robert Monroe is unique among the small number of people who have written about repeated OOBEs, in that he recognizes the extent to which his mind tries to interpret his experiences, to force them into familiar patterns. Thus his accounts are particularly valuable, for he works very hard to try to "tell it like it is."

Another of Mr. Monroe's rare characteristics is his willingness to subject his experiences to critical scrutiny by others, particularly his willingness to work with scientists in investigating his abilities. I am sorry to add that this willingness has been mostly one-sided: I have been the only scientist to take much time to work with him. I shall describe the initial experiments we have been able to carry out together in trying to learn something about both the physiological and parapsychological aspects of his OOBEs. These experiments are only a modest beginning so far, but they add some useful information.

The initial series of laboratory studies we were able to do occurred over a period of several months between September 1965 and August 1966, while I was able to use the facilities of the Electroencephalographic (brain wave) Laboratory of the University of Virginia Medical School.

On eight occasions Mr. Monroe was asked to try to produce an OOBE while hooked up to various instruments for measuring physiological functions. He was also asked to try to direct his movements during the OOBE into the adjoining room, both to observe the activity of the technician monitoring the recording equipment and to try to read a five-digit random target number, which was placed on a shelf six feet above the floor. Measurements were made of Mr. Monroe's brain waves (the electroencephalogram), eye movements, and heart rate (the electrocardiogram).

The laboratory was, unfortunately, not very comfortable for lying still for prolonged periods; we had to bring an army cot into the recording room, as there was no bed there. One of the connections for recording brain waves, the ear electrode, was of a clip type that caused some irritation to the ear, and this made relaxation somewhat difficult.

On the first seven nights during which he attempted to produce an OOBE, Mr. Monroe was not successful. On his eighth night he was able to produce two very brief OOBEs. The first brief OOBE involved witnessing some unrecognized people talking at an unknown location, so there was no way of checking whether it was "fantasy" or a real perception of events happening at a distance. In the second brief OOBE, Mr. Monroe reported he couldn't control his movements very well, so he did not report on the target number in the adjacent room. He did correctly describe that the laboratory technician was out of the room, and that a man (later identified as her husband) was with her in a corridor. As a parapsychologist, I cannot say that this "proves" that Mr. Monroe really knew what was happening at a distance: it is hard to assess the improbability of such an event occurring after the fact. Nevertheless, I found this result quite encouraging for one of the initial attempts to bring such an unusual phenomenon into the laboratory.

Both of these two brief OOBEs occurred in conjunction with brain-wave patterns classified as Stage 1. This is the brain-wave pattern usually occurring in dreaming sleep. In addition, there were some rapid eye movements. Such eye movements also occur during ordinary dreaming sleep, and seem to be a scanning of the dream imagery, i.e., the eyes continue to scan a picture which exists only in the brain in dreams. Heart rate during the OOBEs was quite normal at about sixty-five to seventy beats per minute. At first glance, then, it seems that Mr. Monroe's OOBEs occurred during the same brain state ordinarily associated with Stage 1 dreaming. The main discrepancy with this idea is that Mr. Monroe estimated that each OOBE lasted about thirty seconds, while each period of Stage 1 dreaming lasted about three minutes. Further details can be found in the original publication.[3]

My next opportunity to work with Mr. Monroe in the laboratory came when he visited me in California during the summer of 1968. We were able to have a single laboratory session under much more comfortable circumstances: a normal bed was available, rather than a cot, and we used a different type of electrode for measuring brain waves which was not physically uncomfortable. Under these conditions, Mr. Monroe was able to produce two brief OOBEs.

He awoke almost immediately after the first OOBE had ended, and estimated that it had lasted eight to ten seconds. The brain-wave record just before he awoke again showed a Stage 1 pattern, with possibly a single rapid eye movement occurring during that time. His blood pressure showed a sudden drop, a steady low lasting eight seconds, and a sudden resurgence to normal.

In terms of Mr. Monroe's experience, he reported that he "rolled out" of his body, found himself in the hallway separating his room from the recording room for a few seconds, and then felt a need to get back into his body because of a difficulty in breathing. An assistant, Joan Crawford, and I had been watching him on a closed-circuit television set during this time and we saw him move his arm slightly away from his throat just before he awoke and reported.

Mr. Monroe tried again to produce another OOBE that would be evidential in terms of ESP, coming over and seeing the recording room and reading a target number on a shelf in that room. His brain-wave pattern showed much light sleep, so after three quarters of an hour, I called out to him over the intercom to remind him that we wanted him to try to produce an OOBE. A while later, he reported having produced an OOBE, but being unsure of his orientation, he followed a wire which he thought led to the recording room, and instead found himself outside in a strange area that he never recalled seeing before. He decided he was hopelessly disoriented and came back to his body. His description of that area matched an interior courtyard of the building that he would indeed have found himself in during an OOBE if he had inadvertently gone in exactly the opposite direction he should have. It is not absolutely certain that he had never seen this courtyard while visiting my office earlier in the day, so this experience is not in itself good evidence for a paranormal component to the OOBE.

In terms of physiological changes, he again showed a Stage 1 dreaming pattern, with only two rapid eye movements in the whole period and no clear-cut blood pressure drop on this occasion.

Results to date in the laboratory, then, have recorded the state of Mr. Monroe's brain and body during four brief OOBEs. The general pattern seems to be that they take place in a brain-wave state ordinarily associated with nocturnal dreaming, and that there may sometimes be a blood pressure drop, but no over-all change in heart rate. Certainly I have not seen the "deathlike trance" indicated as being necessary for OOBEs in some of the older occult literature, although such a "trance" might be more characteristic of prolonged OOBEs. On the surface, then, OOBE activity for Mr. Monroe seems to take place when ordinary dreaming would take place in other people. It would be an oversimplification at this time, however, to conclude that his OOBEs are dreams, for several reasons. First, Mr. Monroe sharply distinguishes his experience of dreams from the OOBE experience. Second, he seldom remembers dream experiences since his OOBE experiences began. Third, if we were dealing with a physiological manifestation of an ordinary dream state, I would estimate that we would have far more rapid eye movements than I have seen; that is, if we want to assume that Mr. Monroe's OOBEs are a special sort of dreaming, then the usual relationship between eye movements and dream imagery does not seem to hold up very well. Fourth, Mr. Monroe reports that many of his OOBE experiences have taken place almost immediately after going to bed in the evening; it is extremely rare for ordinary Stage 1 dreaming to occur before subjects have had eighty to ninety minutes of nondreaming sleep. OOBE activity may have substituted for ordinary dreaming here, even though the same or a similar physiological state is utilized.

All the laboratory work with Mr. Monroe up to this point has been very straightforward in conception. I have asked him to produce OOBEs while I measured what happened in his body, with the hope that I might not only understand it but, knowing what the proper bodily conditions were, might be able to produce them in other ways and so induce the experience in others. Parapsychologically, I have asked him to try to read a target number located in another room as straightforward proof that, in some sense, his sensing abilities were "there," rather than restricted to his physical body. He has reported that he hasn't yet been able to control his movements well enough to accomplish the second task, but expects eventually to be able to under laboratory conditions; indeed, a young lady whom I studied was able to do so.* As you will find in reading Mr. Monroe's fascinating book, however, "proof" may not be this simple.

---

*This young lady was quite a different case from Mr. Monroe, as her OOBEs were more accidental, albeit frequent, and she had them in a different brain-wave state than Mr. Monroe. She was, however, able to correctly read a five-digit random number that was placed on a shelf well above her eyesight on one occasion. Complete details may be found in reference 2.

Mr. Monroe's experiences, those of many prominent mystics throughout the ages, and all the data of ESP indicate that our current physical view of the world is a very limited one, that the dimensions of reality are much wider than our current concepts. My attempts and those of other investigators to make these experiences behave in an acceptable fashion may not work out as well as we would like. Let me give two examples of "experiments" with Mr. Monroe which were impressive to me personally, but which are very difficult to evaluate by our ordinary scientific criteria.

Shortly after completing the first series of laboratory experiments, I moved from the east coast to California. A few months after moving, my wife and I decided to set up an experiment. One evening we would concentrate intensely for half an hour, in an attempt to help Mr. Monroe have an OOBE and come to our home. If he were then able to describe our home, this would produce good data on the parapsychological aspects of his OOBEs. I telephoned Mr. Monroe that afternoon, and told him only that we would try to direct him across the country to our home at some unspecified time that night, without giving him any further details.

That evening I randomly selected a time which, I believed, would occur well after Mr. Monroe would be asleep. My random selection came out 11 P.M. California time, or 2 A.M. east coast time. At 11 P.M. my wife and I began our concentration. At 11:05 P.M. the telephone rang, interrupting it. We did not answer the telephone, but tried to continue our concentration until 11:30 P.M. The following morning I telephoned Mr. Monroe and told him only that the results had been encouraging, and that he should write down an independent account of what he had experienced for later comparison against our independent accounts.

On the evening of the experiment, Mr. Monroe had the following experience, which I quote from the notes he mailed me: "Evening passed uneventfully, and I finally got into bed about 1:40 A.M., still wide awake (north-south position). The cat was lying in bed with me. After a long period of calming my mind, a sense of warmth swept over my body, with no break in consciousness, no pre-sleep. Almost immediately, I felt something (or someone) rocking my body from side to side, then tugging at my feet! (I heard the cat let out a complaining yell.) I recognized immediately that this had something to do with Charlie's experiment, and with full trust, did not feel my usual caution (about strangers). The tugging at the legs continued, and I finally managed to separate one Second Body arm, and held it up, feeling around in the dark. After a moment, the tugging stopped, and a hand took my wrist, first gently, then very, very firmly, and pulled me out of the physical easily. Still trusting, and a little excited, I expressed willingness to go to Charlie, if that was where he (it) wanted to lead me. The answer came back affirmatively (although there was no sense of personality, very businesslike). With the hand around my wrist very firmly, I could feel a part of the arm belonging to the hand (slightly hairy, muscular male). But I could not "see" who belonged to the arm. I also heard my name called once.

"Then we started to move, with the familiar feeling of something like air rushing around the body. After a short trip (seemed like five seconds in duration), we stopped and the hand released my wrist. There was complete silence and darkness. Then I drifted down into what seemed to be a room. . . ."

I've stopped quoting from Mr. Monroe's notes at this point, except to add that when he finished this brief trip and got out of bed to telephone me it was 2:05 A.M., his time. Thus the time match with my wife and I beginning to concentrate was extremely good: he felt the tug pulling him from his body within a minute or so of when we started to concentrate. On the other hand, his continuing description of what our home looked like and what my wife and I were doing was not good at all: he "perceived" too many people in the room, he "perceived" me doing things I didn't do, and his description of the room itself was quite vague.

What do I make of this? This is one of those frustrating events that parapsychologists encounter when working with poorly controlled phenomena. It is not evidential enough to say that it was unquestionably a paranormal effect, yet it is difficult simply to say that nothing happened. It is comfortable to stick with our common-sense assumptions that the physical world is what it seems to be, and that a man (or his sense organs) is either located at a certain place and able to observe it or he is not. Some OOBEs reported in the literature seem to fit this view, while others have a disturbing mixture of correct perceptions of the physical situation with "perceptions" of things that weren't there or didn't happen (to us ordinary observers). Mr. Monroe reports a number of such mixed experiences in his book, especially his seeming to "communicate" with people while he is having an OOBE, but their never remembering it.

The second puzzling "experiment" occurred in the fall of 1970 when I briefly visited Mr. Monroe in Virginia, en route to a conference in Washington. Staying overnight, I requested that if he had an OOBE that night, he should come to my bedroom and try to pull me out of my body so I could have the experience too. I realized at the time that I made this request with a certain amount of ambivalence: I wanted him to succeed, yet another part of me did not. More on that later.

Sometime after dawn that morning (I had slept somewhat fitfully and the light was occasionally waking me), I was dreaming when I began vaguely remembering that Mr. Monroe was supposed to try to get me out of my body. I became partially conscious, while remaining in the dream world,* and felt a sense of "vibration" all around me in the dream world, a "vibration" that had a certain amount of indefinable menace connected with it. In spite of the fear this aroused, I thought that I should try to have an OOBE, but at that point I lost my thread of consciousness, and only remember waking up a while later, feeling that the experiment was a failure. A week later I received a letter from a colleague in New York, the well-known parapsychologist Dr. Stanley Krippner, and I began to wonder if it really was a "failure." He was writing to me about an experience his stepdaughter, Carie, who I am quite fond of, had the same morning I was having my "dream." Carie had spontaneously reported to her father that she had seen me in a restaurant in New York City on her way to school that morning. This would have been roughly about the time I was having the dream. Neither she nor her father knew that I was on the east coast.

What do I make of this? This was the first time in years that I had consciously attempted to have an OOBE (I have never, to my knowledge, succeeded), and while I had no conscious memory of having one, a friend reports seeing me in a restaurant in New York City. Even more puzzling, I would have no desire in the world to go to a restaurant in New York City, a place I dislike intensely, if I were having an OOBE, although visiting Carie and her family is always very pleasant. Coincidence? Again, something I would never present as scientific evidence of anything, but something I can't dismiss as meaningless.

This last incident illustrates an attitude toward OOBEs that I have observed in myself, although I do not like to admit it, which is that I am somewhat afraid of them. Part of me is very interested in the phenomenon scientifically, another part of me is excited at the prospect of personally experiencing it. A third part of me knows that an OOBE is something like dying, or opening up part of my mind to an unknown realm, and this third part is not at all anxious to

---

*Becoming aware that one is dreaming has been used as a technique for inducing OOBEs, as well as being interesting in its own right. See reference 1 for material on such "lucid" dreams.

get on with it. *If* OOBEs are "real," *if* the things Mr. Monroe describes cannot be dismissed as an interesting kind of fantasy or dream, our world view is going to change radically. And uncomfortably.

One thing that psychologists are reasonably sure of about human nature is that it resists change. We like the world to be the way we think it is, even if we think it's unpleasant. At least we can anticipate what may happen. Change and uncertainty have possibilities of unsettling things happening, especially when that change doesn't take account of our desires, our wills, our egos.

REFERENCES

1. Tart, C.: *Altered States of Consciousness: A Book of Readings.* New York: John Wiley & Sons, 1969.
2. Tart, C.: A psychophysiological study of out-of-the-body experiences in a selected subject. *J. Am. Soc. Psychical Res.*, 62:3–27, 1968.
3. Tart, C.: A second psychophysiological study of out-of-the-body experiences in a gifted subject. *Int. J. Parapsychology*, 9:251–258, 1967.

Chapter 8

Potential of the Sport Experience

Kenneth Ravizza

I never played basketball like that before; there was such an incredible feeling of control, strength, flow, and inner power as I drove to the basket. I knew I could do anything I wanted on the court. Nothing was resisting me as I moved effortlessly in toward the basket again and again. There was no distinction between myself, the ball, and the basket—we all were together.

These were some of the feelings I had while practicing basketball all alone on a deserted playground court at the age of thirteen. It began on one particular drive toward the basket in which I drove around four giant imaginary defensive players, stopped, faked right, and shot the ball to the left. After that drive, things just started to fall into place and my driving got more and more intense. I would drive in, go through my various movements, shoot the ball, and then bring it out and drive in again. I did not think about anything; I just moved with the ball in a way that I never previously had.

I am still not certain of the exact duration of this experience for I was so involved that I lost track of the time. Time was not relevant to me; playing with that ball and leaping effortlessly toward the hoop were all that mattered. After a while, I stopped and I was not certain what had occurred, but I definitely knew it was something very special for me. I had never realized that I could move with a basketball like that, consequently, I experienced a real boost of confidence from this new knowledge of my capabilities. I can still recall walking home with a feeling of being totally satisfied and proud of my abilities, which was reflected by a large smile on my face, radiating with an intense joy. This experience has always retained a special meaning for me. Whenever I think about it I can put myself right back there and reflect on some of the great feelings that I had.

About 10 years later when I was a graduate student, I was reading the book *Toward A Psychology of Being* by psychologist Abraham Maslow in which he developed the concept of the peak-experience. It was a generalization of the greatest moments of life, of experiences of fantastic joy, bliss, ecstasy, and sheer delight. When I reflected on experiences I had that were similiar to his description, my playground basketball experience immediately came to mind. That was an experience that really stood out for me, and I viewed it as a personal treasure that provided incredible meaning for my lifelong love of sport. As I reflected on Maslow's concept I thought of all the time that athletes dedicate to sport, and it appeared likely that many athletes have similiar experiences that really stand out for them. Becoming intrigued with this area, I talked with other athletes to learn if they had enjoyed similiar experiences. I was surprised to find that most of them could recall a sport experience radiating the same kind of intensity as my own basketball experience. At this point I began an in-depth reading of Maslow's work to obtain a clearer understanding of this type of phenomenon.

Maslow described the peak-experience as a moment in which the individual experiences total happiness, a loss of the fears, inhibitions, weaknesses, and insecurities that often plague most of us. In addition, peak-experiences are moments of great maturity, fulfillment, individuality, or the healthiest moments for the individual in the sense that he may feel the total unity, inner strength, and wholeness of his being. The person experiences a total fascination and awe of the matter at hand, as though he were "lost" in the experience.

A central point pertaining to the peak-experience is that it is a transient experience—a temporary phenomenon analogous to a gentle summer breeze which comes and goes. Maslow referred to the peak-experience as being similiar to a temporary trip to heaven. "I have likened the peak-experience in a metaphor to a personally defined heaven from which the person then returns to earth."[4]

Briefly, then, the peak-experience can be denoted to mean a particular experience in which the individual has an ecstatic, nonvoluntary, transient experience of being totally integrated, at peace with himself, functioning fully, and in complete control of the situation. Frank Goble, in his book *The Third Force*, makes the following comparison, "... with an engine that suddenly hits all cylinders and performs perfectly, producing a real surge of power, whereas it had been missing, sputtering, and running poorly."[1]

From the aforementioned description, one might assume that in order to undergo a peak-experience the individual would have to take up residence in an Ashram in Tibet, go in the mountains and meditate, or sit under a tree and ponder the great truths; Maslow, however, did not find this to be the case. He believed that these experiences were natural.

> *They don't necessarily take years of training or study. They are not restricted to far-out people, i.e., to monks, saints, or yogis, Zen Buddhists, Orientals, or people in any special state of grace. It is not something that happens in the Far East, in special places, or to specially trained and chosen people. It's available in the midst of life to everyday people in everyday occupations.*[3]

He also pointed out the conditions and sources of peak-experiences.

> *. . . the sacred is in the ordinary, that it is, to be found in one's daily life, in one's neighbors, friends and family, in one's backyard, and travel may be a flight from confronting the sacred. . . .*[4]

The peak-experience is common to all places and times and people. One may liken the peak-experience to the Oriental concept of Nirvana, which is not a future location like heaven that one may go to after death, but rather is the "here and now." Simply stated, we do not have to die to experience the heaven within us. This type of experience is not unique to modern man. It has been with human beings since antiquity. Almost every culture and religion refer to this type of experience. St. Paul called it the "peace that passeth understanding," Zen Buddhists, the term "satori" or "kensho," and Yoga, "moksha." Taoists use the term "the absolute Tao" and the Quakers coined the expression of the "inner light" to represent these moments.[8]

It is important to realize that the peak-experience is natural, and not a supernatural experience with strict dogma accompanying it. In reference to the origins of peak-experiences, Maslow stated:

> *They came from the great moments of love and sex, from the great moments (particularly of music), from the bursts of creativeness, and the creative furore (the great inspiration), from great moments of insight and of discovery . . . from certain athletic experiences.*[3]

As Maslow stated, the "sacred is in the ordinary," so it follows that the sport experience provides an environment for this type of highly subjective phenomenon. As he explained: "The love for the body, awareness of the body—these are clearly good paths to peak-experiences."[2]

Sport provides an environment in which one can become totally engrossed in the activity that one is participating in. Sport has a "special air" to it: there is a set time to play, a specified area to perform within, and specific rules that must be followed. There is also a score to which we can refer in order to observe how well we are doing in relation to the other participants. How often in our daily lives do we find things this precise and well defined? Usually our lives are cluttered with ambiguity, whereas sport provides us with an explicit structure which creates an atmosphere in which we can transcend the mundane daily problems, such as earning money, preparing for exams, keeping up with inflation. Because the rules provide all the guidelines and structure, one is free to focus all of one's energies on the well-defined task at hand and go all out to pursue the desired objectives. This may result in an explosion of man's energy on one specific task for a specified time, and it often becomes an explosion of sheer joy. This all-out effort may provide the athlete with a new personal knowledge of his potential in that specific activity.

In addition, participation in sport is freely chosen by the athlete, he is not compelled to participate. Because it is voluntary he is more apt to become involved, since he always has the prerogative to drop out at any point. As David Reisman stated: "Play may prove to be the sphere in which there is still room left for would-be autonomous man to reclaim his individual character from the pervasive demands of his social character."[6] In playing sport, the individual may have a multitude of subjective experiences that turn him on to the sport experience, and most importantly, make him aware of the outer reaches of himself as a moving person. The peak-experience is one of the experiences that may provide the athlete with significant insights into his sport participation, and his life in general. Sport definitely has unlimited meaning for the participating athlete; why else would he expend so much time and energy? It is this dedication to sport that allows him to get totally wrapped up in it and enjoy the intensity of the peak-experience.

THE PEAK-EXPERIENCE

Many researchers in physical education and sport have referred to the fantastic affective experiences which sport provides the athlete, but few have offered a specific explanation as to what these experiences felt like to the athletes. For this reason, I wanted to interview athletes in order to ascertain their subjective experiences. What were their feelings during their greatest moments *while* actually participating in sport? I interviewed 20 athletes who had participated at all levels, from informal jogging to Olympic competition. The interviews lasted from one to two hours, and I attempted to grasp an understanding of the person's experience *while* participating in sport.[7]

The athletes recalled that they were so involved in the experience that they lost sight of the "normal" conscious self. Some athletes went further—their involvement caused them to become one with the experience. In other words, they experienced such an integration and unity with the activity that they no longer perceived a distinction between the experience and the "self." A woman discus thrower explained: "I became the motion, for all purposes I was motion." From the interviews, I discovered 13 closely related qualities that the athletes shared during their greatest moments while participating in sport.

A UNIQUE EXPERIENCE FOR THE ATHLETE

The sport peak-experience is unique—it stands apart from normal daily living and the usual involvement in sport. The uniqueness may be attributed to the intensity or quality of the experience. Often, there is an "ecstatic shock" associated with the phenomenon. A swimmer noted: "This was a whole new experience for me. I never did anything to this degree before. There is no way this could happen again." If the sport peak-experience is not unique, it would become common, and if the phenomenon occurs frequently, then it would not stand out. This does not mean, however, that the circumstances or the sport environment need be out of the ordinary for the peak-experience to occur. The uniqueness lies in the way that one experiences the phenomenon, and it is this uniqueness that often makes it a personal treasure, greater than any trophy.

NONVOLUNTARY EXPERIENCE

An athlete cannot control or determine when the peak-experience will occur. It can be compared to a sudden breeze on a calm and sultry day which stirs the garments and refreshes the spirit, but nothing one consciously does can make it return. The athlete, however, may set the stage for the phenomenon by getting into the necessary physical and mental condition. This is accomplished by totally engrossing himself in the experience, and doing whatever he needs to do to be open to the experience. Yet, even this will not guarantee a peak-experience. As a cyclist so appropriately explained: "I am a vehicle for this (peak-experience), I initiate the performance and then the experience takes over."

TEMPORARY EXPERIENCE

The peak-experience in sport is a transient experience, it comes and it goes, yet it can always be remembered. Although an individual has a peak-experience, after a time the intensity of the experience subsides and things return to "normal."

TEMPORARY TRANSCENDENCE OF NORMAL CHARACTERISTICS OF SELF

There are seven qualities of the peak-experience that are closely interrelated with each other and contrasted with the normal everyday characteristics of the self. Each of these qualities contributes to the other qualities in a unique way, and thus they are presented under this one heading of temporary transcendence.

Temporary Transcendence of Self. An essential characteristic of the sport peak-experience is a *temporary transcendence of self.* In this sense, transcendence means that the athlete experiences himself in a different manner from the usual one, because in the sport peak-experience there is a *harmony, oneness, or totality* to the phenomenon that normally is not present in the sport experience. A characteristic of this harmony or oneness is the individual's union with an object, himself, or the environment. A cyclist described this harmony: "I am at one with everything. There is no distinction between myself, the bicycle, the track, speed, or anything. There is a oneness with everything." Some athletes talked about it in terms of temporal and spatial changes, whereas others mentioned feelings of oneness, harmony, and being all together. A football player explained: "You forget who you are for a while. Have you ever been so high while doing something that you forget where and who you are? It's as though you're someone else." The athlete is no longer a separate self looking at the world. Rather, he merges with the phenomenon and forms a oneness with the experience.

Total Engrossment. During its duration, the athlete finds himself completely absorbed in the experience. This *total immersion* results in the athlete centering all his energy, attention, and even his being on the sport experience. When the athlete is consciously thinking about how to catch a football, or the feeling he experiences while catching the ball, he cannot be totally involved with experience, because part of himself remains on the periphery of the experience, cognizing about what is happening and thereby distracting him from the experience. As a football player stated: "I concentrate my whole being on one thing: this is one of the few times I have done this. . . . I am just hitting him (the ball carrier) and nothing else." Once the athlete thinks about the experience, be it execution or feelings, he becomes an object of his experience and thus breaks the union that was formed.

Narrow Focus of Attention. Another aspect of this transcendence, similar to being totally engrossed in the experience, is that during the sport peak-experience the athlete's focus of attention is narrow, and many of the usual thoughts of the athlete such as what is the score or how well he is doing are absent. Thus, the athlete narrows his focus on the sport activity, involves himself in the experience, and is in harmony with it.

The athletes described how they focused their total energy and awareness on the particular movement experience and became an integral part of the activity. A lacrosse player explained: "It is a world within a world—focused right there. I am not aware of the external. My concentration is so great I don't think of anything else."

Everything is Perfect. During the peak-experience in sport, everything is experienced just as it "should" be; all the athletes claimed they would not alter any aspect of the experience. A football player explained: "Everything is right, everything is in line, everything is clicking, nothing is opposing me." It is one of those few times that everything is perfect—nothing distracts the athlete.

Total Control. During the sport peak-experience, the individual is at his or her fullest potential and feels in *total control* of the situation. All the athletes reported this quality of being in control, however, they discussed it in two different ways. Some athletes felt in control of the situation and made reference to its importance. A swimmer stated: "There was a complete and fluid control of my body. In the last part of the race I was in total control. There was no pain. I was in control of the water and my total bodily actions." This feeling of being at the height of one's power, or invincible, provides the athlete with a feeling of control over whatever may confront him. A football player revealed: "Things were under control; my body could do anything . . . it was almost as though my body was not there. Nothing out there could in any way affect me. I could do anything I wanted."

The second way in which the athletes discussed control was explained by a cyclist: "I don't think about it or attempt to control it." It is pertinent to take note that this cyclist experienced a total blackness during his peak-experience. I asked him how he kept his bike on the track if all he observed was blackness, and he explained: "I can just tell where I am . . . the situation is in control, not me. I experience a freedom in that I do nothing because it is happening." Things are perfect as they are and there is no need to control them. Control in this second sense is more a feeling of being an integral part of the situation and thus consistent and integrated with what is happening, rather than of manipulating or consciously attempting to control the situation.

Total Loss of Fear. Associated with perfection and control is a total loss of fear, particularly fear of failure that is so common in athletics. Because everything is going perfectly and everything is under control there is nothing to fear.

Effortless Movement. Since the individual temporarily transcends himself, the movement becomes effortless. One no longer has to consciously exert oneself, one just moves. A football player reflected upon the incredible ease of a particular block: "So many times I put everything into it but nothing happens. But this time I hit him just right and everything went perfectly. It was effortless . . . I hit him and he just flew. Physically, I didn't put as much as usual into it." During a peak-experience, there is no awareness of the techniques or the pains involved in the moving that the usual self may experience. The athlete does not have to force his movements; he just moves as though something or someone were moving him. If the athlete had to be continuously exerting himself, he would not be able to fuse totally with the experience, because there would always be that segment of his self that would be separated from the whole by continuously providing the motivation.

SELF-VALIDATING EXPERIENCE

All of the athletes interviewed agreed that the sport peak-experience is a self-validating phenomenon. The experience is total, complete, self-validating, and independent of external circumstances. A woman volleyball player addressed this quality when she stated: "The experience is in the process while participating. It sometimes happens that the end result may distract from it, but it remains valid." In all cases, the athlete knew he had had a great experience. Even if the contest or game was lost, the experience itself possessed a beauty, wonder, and uniqueness that made the final score irrelevant.

BASIC SKILL LEVEL

Essential to the sport peak-experience is the ability of the athlete to execute the basic skill without having to worry about his technique. Unless the athlete has a complete mastery of the basic skills, he will be too preoccupied with the fundamentals to be totally involved with the experience.

The athlete does not have to be an expert with years of experience, although in some sports it might take that long to develop the necessary skills. Briefly, the athlete should be comfortable with and in control of the fundamental techniques. For example, a beginning skier must be conscious of every shift in body weight and must constantly anticipate his next movement. Only after he no longer has to mentally contrive his next movement can he hope to experience a peak-experience while skiing.

The peak-experience is a subjective event that is unique, nonvoluntary, and transient. At this heightened moment of awareness, the athlete experiences a oneness or union with the activity. With this union is a temporary transcendence of the normal self into an integrated relationship with the experience. The athlete intuits that everything is perfect; the effortless feeling of being in total control of the situation permeates the experience. The usual fears and anxieties that may accompany the activity are forgotten and all that matters is the moment and just "doing it."

PERSONAL INSIGHTS

From my exploration of the peak-experience, I have become aware of the further reaches that sport participation may make available to the athlete, and I will share some of the insights that I have gained from this research. What do we mean when we say that someone is a success in sport? So often one's immediate connotation is that the person or team won the game or broke a record. Winning has become the major criterion to measure "success." All you have to do is look at the sport pages in most newspapers to observe this.

A sport participant does not have to be playing at an advanced level of competition or in front of a crowd to have this type of experience. Once an athlete has developed the basic skills that are essential to the activity, he is capable of becoming totally involved in the activity, which is a necessary characteristic for the peak-experience to occur. This experience may happen in any sport activity and at any level of competition, even in a physical education class. This has pertinent implications for coaches, because during the sport peak-experience the athlete's performance may not merit a victory as far as the score or time is concerned, yet the athlete may have a peak-experience in the process of playing and this is a special type of victory that should be acknowledged.

The subjective experience does not necessarily have to approach the intensity of the peak-experience to make it meaningful. I was surprised to discover that most of the athletes I interviewed did not share their greatest moments (in sport) with other people. They could share the winning performance but not the feelings that accompanied it. As a runner stated: "I would have been laughed at by my friends. Maybe a close friend would be able to understand, but it is not too masculine to think of these things."

The subjective domain in sport is frequently neglected by coaches. So often coaches are too busy preparing for the next game to discuss or to make the athletes aware of the subjective domain. They spend hours improving the athlete's performance, but the experiential areas of sport are neglected, and these are the very areas that provide the athlete with his or her own personal meaning. How many times have you been on a team when a period was set aside to discuss the feelings you had while participating? We make fantastic claims about sport being "educational." What can be more educational than the knowledge one gains from the subjective area and the peak-experience specifically? We leave it up to the athlete to determine the ramifications of his experiences in sport. To me this is too important an area to leave to chance. We can encourage athletes to recognize and discuss their subjective experiences just as we help them to improve their performance.

The sport peak-experience provides the athlete with a unique experience in which he accepts his body, his participation, and his movement as one entity. His muscles are no longer perceived as antagonistic, the effortless qualities just take over. Many athletes revealed that their sport peak-experiences provided them with new dimensions to their sport participation and opened new and significant personal knowledge. This is an important part of the educational experience that sport provides. A new type of education is discussed by Frank Goble when he states: "This education will put more emphasis on the development of the person's potential, particularly the potential to be human, to understand the self and others and to relate to them, to achieve the basic human needs, to grow toward self-actualization. This education will help the person to become the best that he is able to become."[1]

The sport experience definitely provides an ambience in which the athlete can reach his fullest potential and develop the human qualities. We can contribute to this understanding by taking the extra time to aid the athlete to explore the subjective domain. Specifically, the peak-experience is one occasion during which the athlete experiences himself to the fullest and gains the personal knowledge that comes with this. Such an experience allows the athlete to understand his capabilities as never before. Not only can an individual benefit from this view of himself as a moving being, but also he may be able to gain personal insight to his potential as a human being outside the realm of sport.

If only athletes could feel comfortable in sharing their subjective experiences with other members of the team, it would help to bring the team together. Such an approach would strengthen team bonds; victory would be one goal and personal expression of a meaningful experience would be another. Traditionally, victory is the major cause for celebration in sport; however, if subjective experiences were regarded as highly as winning, team members would realize the value of their assistance to another person, thereby uniting the team at still another level.

From subjective study, one gains insights into the total sport experience. We know that the peak-experience in sport is a unique, transient, nonvoluntary, and transcending phenomenon. As a result of it, the athlete begins to observe new horizons and diverse meanings in the sport experience. Clearly, sport is one domain in which the participants can experience themselves to their fullest possible limits and go on to greater self-knowledge.

REFERENCES

1. Goble, F.: *The Third Force*. New York: Simon and Schuster, Inc., 1971.
2. Maslow, A.: *The Farther Reaches of Human Nature*. New York: Viking Press, 1971.
3. Maslow, A.: Lessons from peak-experiences. *J. Human. Psychol.*, 2:9–18, 1967.
4. Maslow, A.: *Religions, Values and Peak-Experiences*. New York: Viking Press, 1964.
5. Maslow, A.: *Toward A Psychology of Being*, 2nd ed. New York, Von Nostrand Reinhold Company, 1968.
6. Miller, D. M., and Russell, K.: *Sport: A Contemporary View*. Philadelphia: Lea & Febiger, 1971.
7. Ravizza, K.: A Study of the Peak-Experience in Sport. Unpublished doctoral dissertation. Los Angeles, Calif.: University of Southern California, 1973.
8. White, J. (Ed.): *The Highest State of Consciousness*. New York: Doubleday and Co., Inc., 1972.

Chapter 9

Beautiful, Just Beautiful

Carolyn E. Thomas

There are many ways in which it is possible to view sport as an aesthetic experience, and the literature shows the beginning of a number of attempts to view sport in such a way. Examples may be found in the writings of Kaelin,[2] Osterhoudt,[6] Thomas,[7,8] Keenan,[3] Fisher,[1] Ziff,[9] and Kuntz.[4] Two basic ways to view sport, art, or any life experience seem to be developing. One is from the perspective of the audience and the other is from the perspective of the performer. Nietzsche has most notably classified these two perspectives as Dionysian and Apollonian. The Apollonian perspective is primarily the spectator view, characterized by cognitive objectivity, criticism, logic, and what is commonly called "scientific method." The Dionysian perspective is the performer's orientation, characterized by subjective, spontaneous, and somewhat irrational analysis of performance. The former stems from the spectator's ability to remove himself from the *actual* experience in order to analyze the quantitative and some of the qualitative aspects of the whole experience as it unfolds before him—an "outside-in" view. The second orientation is possible only by the performer who is involved in what is called the "lived experience"—an "inside-out" view. Although the Apollonian and Dionysian perspectives provide distinctly different kinds of information, it is possible for us to view them as providing varying degrees of epistemic correlation. In many respects, they provide complementary data which can serve to enlarge one's understanding of a given phenomenon.

Sociologically, we are primarily concerned with the audience's perspective, that is, how the spectator views the ongoing event, and what meanings, aesthetic or otherwise, the events have in the broad and objective context of society. Psychologically, we are more concerned with the performer's perspective, that is, how the individual perceives his own behavior and his own experience in an event. What meanings, aesthetic and otherwise, do such experiences have in the specific and subjective context of a given individual?

In the examination of the psychological dimension of the aesthetic experience, it can be noted that aside from the traditional connotation of aesthetic meaning beautiful, which is certainly appropriate in the spectator's perspective, the aesthetic experience from the performer's perspective takes on many of the characteristics of Maslow's "peak-experience." This is not to suggest that the two are synonymous or that they should be examined for the same purposes. But for the benefit of definition of an experientially based aesthetic experience, the characteristics of Maslow's peak-experience come close to what we are discussing in terms of a performer's perspective of aesthetics in sport.

For a number of years we have attempted to explain the "why" of physical activity with what might be termed "how" methods. That is, we have used Apollonian and scientific means in an effort to attach meaning and significance to man's participation in sport. Because it is known that behavior is precipitated by the meaningfulness of an act, it would seem both necessary and important for sport philosophers and psychologists to attempt to ascertain more accurately the "why" dimension of sport. However, it may be possible to examine both the peak-experience and the aesthetic experience in hopes of shedding some light on various behavior in sport, as well as of potentially providing an understanding of why people choose to engage in physical activities, often at great physical and psychological expense. To feel or describe without an experiential referent is a sterile symbol of an *idea* of a feeling or an experience. And, although the *actual* participation in sport transcends intellectualization, we know that there are reasons why man chooses sport as a form of human expression. These reasons and this expression would seem to manifest themselves in those moments of extremes and ultimates that have been called "peak-experiences" and/or "aesthetic experiences." It seems appropriate, then, to examine these kinds of experiences, despite the limitations of language, in an attempt to better understand the human expression man seeks in sport.

Peak-experiences and aesthetic experiences are a realization that "what ought to be" is. In the Heideggerian sense, it is a coming into authenticity. These experiences are unique and almost mystic. Although occurring in a spatial-temporal setting, these peak-experiences and/or aesthetic experiences are characterized by a disorientation in space and time. "In the creative furor the poet or artist becomes oblivious of his surroundings and the passage of time."[5] The same can be said for the athlete. The experience is intrinsically valid, perfect, and complete. It is sufficient in itself and needs nothing else. It is felt to be intrinsically necessary and inevitable, as good as it should be. *Perhaps, most importantly, the aesthetic experience in the psychological sense is realized in the feelings of peace and beauty when sport meets man's intents and needs, expresses and fulfills his motivations and dreams, and brings him closer to knowing the reasons why he plays.*

Art, like sport, has both the spectator and the performer dimensions, and the audience can have an aesthetic experience listening to a symphony or viewing a painting, dance, or drama. Kaelin suggests that the audience at a sporting event can experience a sense of drama in the closely matched contest, and that the contest then takes on aesthetic qualities. The "beauty" of the well-skilled athletic body in motion has, for many spectators, aesthetic overtones. This seems to be particularly true for sports—gymnastics, diving, synchronized swimming, figure skating—in which the human body, rather than an implement, is the primary focus. However, the "fit" and well-skilled body in motion, executing a series of perfected skills, is, for some, a beautiful event to watch regardless of the activity.

Little has been written about the aesthetic experience that the artist has during periods of creating a work of art. Equally little has been written about the performer's perception of the sport experience. Most of what we know about an individual's perceptions of sport experiences comes from the athlete's introspective accounts of his feelings about his experiences. However subjective and unscientific such data may be, they remain the only means of gaining insight into experience from the performer's perspective, because no spectator, regardless of empathy, can be in the performer's role, and no performer, given his commitment to the ongoing experience, has been able to remove himself cognitively from the ongoing experience to describe it as it is occurring. Few performers strive for academic revelation in their analysis or descriptions. Rather, such descriptions are often stated in simple language free from jargon and analogy, which is perhaps indicative of a basic, direct, and uncomplicated experience. Yet it is clear that *what* they describe is somehow close and meaningful to them. The *why* of the experience may be more remote and/or unimportant for many athletes than the *what*, and the interpretation of *what* they say into the *why* is being undertaken by sport philosophers and sport psychologists. This, of course, is not without some risk of misinterpretation, because the interpreter is necessarily in the

Apollonian domain and has no basis for entering *in* to the *actual* experience.

I would like to synthesize some of the many comments that have been descriptive of the sport experience. The attitudes presented here are not intended to represent all attitudes, but seem to be those that recur in the verbal and written accounts given by athletes about their sport experiences. I hope these eclectic characterizations will reflect some of the attitudes athletes have about their performance. It will be apparent that, although some athletes are inattentive to body and feeling cues, others are most sensitive to the totality of the sport experience. Examination of a range of attitudes may provide some insights into the psychological conditioning athletes receive early in their sport experiences. I will intentionally be brief and incomplete in the presentation and development of these attitudinal positions, hoping that *each* reader will critically add and develop for himself the potential that the attitudes have for our study of sport. Keep in mind also that the attitudes are somewhat like somatotypes, in that few athletes will fit clearly and only into one attitude. Let us suppose we are talking to players of a winning team (although it could be a losing team with some modifications in interpretations) after a difficult season-ending victory, and the players are giving their immediate perceptions of the game in answer to some unheard questions.

The first attitude carries with it an implied dualism and reveres the "beauty" of the body.

> *Yeah, we were really in shape for this one. Everyone was healthy and we were the strongest we've been all season. The coaches have really whipped us into great physical condition, and we've been working for this one all season. You know you finally work out all the bugs and the plays and everything just comes automatic. We're number one because we're just tougher and strong and we wanted it, that's all. It just all came together, you know, execution and everything. Had some really beautiful moves and we just outlasted 'em.*

There is an indication in this kind of sentiment that it is the physical man who eventually wins out in sport. The well-honed body demonstrates *its* superiority, and because of the body's efficiency and dependability, the athlete can view his body as a beautiful thing which works for him. In a sense, the body is a lovely piece of machinery which is somehow separated from the athlete's selfhood. Nonetheless, many athletes subconsciously take a spectator's perspective when it comes to the idea that the healthy and skilled body is a beautiful and aesthetically pleasing product which should emerge victorious if justice is to prevail.

The second attitude reflects the loss of "I" in the intricacies of teamwork.

> *Coach really got us ready for this one. He had them scouted and we worked all week against their offenses and defenses picking out their weaknesses. You can't hardly miss with preparation like that. . . . Yeah, sure I did my job pretty good today but without the other guys you can't do much, you know. Everybody's got to pull together and do.their part for it to work. Coach knew when to pull guys out so we could keep things moving. . . . Yeah, I guess I did pass my own record but you don't do something like that alone, you know. It's a beautiful thing to work with such a great bunch of guys and it's even better when you can break the big ones like this.*

There appears here almost the sense of self-deprecation, the reluctance to examine one's own experience for either its positive or negative aspects. The individual's identity becomes a part of a much larger identity. The team, because the members function so well together, becomes the source of satisfaction, oneness, mutuality, beauty, and positive feeling in the sport experience. Individual performance is a part of group performance and many share its positive and negative aspects. Again, this takes on the spectator dimension, because the team and its productivity become the things that are viewed. Harmony, balance, integration, symmetry, all become the elements to be scrutinized. When all the elements blend, we seem to have a beautifully moving collective entity.

The third attitude points toward external motivation and evaluation.

> *We really put it to 'em, didn't we? I just hope all the fans were pleased with what we did out there today. We've been getting some real bad press lately and it's kinda hard to knock yourself out and have people booing. We really wanted to play well today 'cause there have been a lot of people who have stuck with*

> *the team all year. This was the game that brings out a*
> *lot of the scouts, and some of the guys were out to look*
> *good since it's their last shot. I'm just real glad we*
> *could pull it off so well for everyone.*

Although the aesthetic dimension is missing here, I point out this attitude to note that seldom can the performer evaluate his performance authentically if the motivations for playing and the criteria for evaluation are external to his own needs and feelings. If the reason "I" play is not for myself, or at least for myself as part of a team, but for others, then the difficulty in the assessing or understanding of personal experience becomes difficult. In the Dionysian perspective, "I" is a presupposition. In the Apollonian, "they" or "it" is a presupposition. Because the performer cannot place himself in the audience during the performance, and if he chooses to play for "they" reasons rather than "I" reasons, the examination of the player's experience by himself or by others is fraught with error. The possibility for an aesthetic experience is impossible if the intent for playing excludes the basic fact that the player is playing for himself, to meet his own needs and to express his own feelings and uniqueness.

The fourth attitude centers on the subjective and egocentric perception of the experience.

> *I really had a good time. There were a couple of plays*
> *when everything was altogether and it was a great*
> *feeling to have accomplished what was planned. I*
> *really wanted to better last season's mark and I feel*
> *real good—I even remember the play. Beautiful, just*
> *beautiful! It was sort of a relief in a way, but when I*
> *knew it had happened it was really clear to me. I felt*
> *excited and peaceful all at once, you know what I*
> *mean? Then everyone was cheering and slapping me*
> *on the back and I came back down to earth. I could go*
> *that route again, you know what I mean?*

There are, in the most recent biographical literature of athletes, usually those in individual and outdoor pursuits, these kinds of attempts to get at a certain moment of the entire experience that stands out as being meaningful or significant. The reasons and the motivations may differ, yet for these athletes there is something about the experience that has made it exceptional. Something has made it unique enough to remember and to want to relive. It is quite personal, taking on the Dionysian modality and becoming difficult to explain to an audience, which may have viewed the same act as routine or even mundane and emotionally unmoving. There is in this attitude a total lack of concern for audience and/or for team. In fact, many of the sports in which this attitude occurs are nonaudience kinds.

The fifth and last attitude we will examine shows a concern for the struggle.

> *You know, they played real well out there today. But I guess that's to be expected. They're usually up for us—gave us some real tense moments. I kinda like that though—keeps you on your toes. No way it was dull—you never know what's gonna happen or how it's gonna go from one play to the next. I think it brings out the best in both teams and makes you really put things altogether to deliver. At least when you get done, you really know you've played a game and you know who's better.*

There is inherent in this attitude an enjoyment of the good fight, an appreciation for the basic nature of competition, a sense of drama that will somehow build to a climactic and justifiable conclusion. The losers played well, but today the better man won unless, of course, we introduced elements of tragedy, fate, or mysticism over which the player-actors had no control. There is also implicit in this attitude a sense of "I" needing a testing ground, a need for the "good hurt," something to press me to my limits to see what I can do, and then my being able to evaluate the experience in some meaningful way. It is a need that takes on a sense of beauty during fulfillment.

With the realization that none of the previous conjecture about attitudes and aesthetics would withstand theoretical testing in logic or conceptual analysis, your critical perceptions should be added to what has been stated here merely as an introductory exploration of the connection between psychology and aesthetics. On the basis of your own sport experience, eliminate the things that create dissonance, and supplement those that allow for congruence. Art is a cherished part of almost every known culture. Man seeks beauty and the aesthetic experience, as spectator and as performer, in the simplicity of nature and in the complexity of structural forms. He has created forms to communicate symbolically, to express his feelings and the feelings of the society around him. He has created forms that meet his needs. In a society where alienation, loneliness, and depression are increasing social phenomena, we find people drawn to sport. We find them seeking activities in which there is some degree of meaning. If sport and man's behavior in sport and because of sport could not be viewed as a meaningful dimension of his existence, it would seem to be extremely difficult to explain the way sport, in both its Apollonian and Dionysian modes, permeates our social structure. I think it is possible now to view sport as a meaningful form in which man seeks and has sought that which is beautiful about himself and his existence. The attitudes exist if we listen carefully to what athletes are saying about their experiences and if we examine our own behavior in sport. The theories and methodologies will come later, therefore let us begin our study of the expression and experience of beauty in sport in open speculation about what we can see and feel from both the Apollonian and Dionysian perspectives of sport.

REFERENCES

1. Fisher, M.: Sport as an aesthetic experience. In *Sport and the Body*. Edited by E. W. Gerber. Philadelphia: Lea & Febiger, 1972.
2. Kaelin, E.: The well-played game: Notes toward an aesthetics of sport. *Quest, X:* 16–28, 1968.
3. Keenan, F.: The athletic contest as a tragic form of art. In *The Philosophy of Sport*. Edited by R. G. Osterhoudt. Springfield, Ill.: Charles C Thomas, 1970.
4. Kuntz, P. G.: Aesthetics applies to sports as well as to the arts. *Philosophic Exchange*, 1:25–40, 1974.
5. Maslow, A.: *Toward a Psychology of Being*. New York: Van Nostrand, 1963.
6. Osterhoudt, R. G.: An Hegelian interpretation of art, sport and athletics. In *The Philosophy of Sport*. Edited by R. G. Osterhoudt. Springfield, Ill.: Charles C Thomas, 1973.
7. Thomas, C. E.: Toward an experiential sport aesthetic. *Philosophic Exchange*, 1:49–64, 1974.
8. Thomas, C. E.: The Perfect Moment: A Sport Aesthetic. Unpublished doctoral dissertation. Columbus, Ohio: The Ohio State University, 1972.
9. Ziff, P.: A fine forehand. *Philosophic Exchange*, 1:41–48, 1974.

Chapter 10

Spirituality and Sport

C. Peggy Gazette

Margaret A. Hukill

Current interest in many of the ancient sports of Eastern cultures presents a timely challenge to physical educators. Hundreds of persons in the United States today are seeking personal benefits and involvement in Asian-originated sports such as aikido, iaido, kendo, judo, karate, Japanese archery, and Yoga. What are these contemporary adherents of ancient sports seeking—physical fitness, self-defense, emotional and spiritual growth, personal enlightenment, a more total life experience?

Beyond the obvious physical and self-defense benefits that can be derived from these Asian sports, one finds a hidden core of "spirituality" that offers balance and gives a deeper meaning to movement. In pure form, a spiritual quality in sport activities can be outwardly observed in the personal centering provided for in rituals before and after an event. Each contestant strives, through a brief meditation period, to attain calmness, enlightenment, and blessing in his search for physical perfection.

Examples of spirituality can be found in many Asian cultures, such as Japanese culture in which the basic philosophy of Zen Buddhism has penetrated many aspects of Japanese life—sports, the theater, flower arrangement, the traditional tea ceremony, and religion. Zen, meaning meditation, emphasizes being in harmony with the cosmos or achieving "oneness" with nature. The concept or spirit of Zen philosophy encompasses a "flowing with the stream of life," a "middle way" approach to living, or even a "stoop to conquer" reflection. The early adherents of Zen sought spiritual enlightenment through extreme physical discipline and mental concentration. According to Reischauer, Zen contributed much to the development of a strength of character, sense of discipline, and inner toughness characteristic of the Japanese today.[4]

Before participation in the ancient forms of self-defense, Japanese tradition provides a moment of meditation for each person to become "centered" with the situation and with himself. From such "centeredness," it is hoped that one's best and total self will emerge. The opponent too, is respected by offering formal bows and salutes prior to competition as well as after the bout. Honoring self as well as the worthy opponent brings to sport a spiritual quality that recognizes the significance of human interplay. During combat, the opponents strive to be aware of each other's actions and moods, so as to move in harmony with the attack rather than to offer resistance of a vigorous strain. This yielding, softness if you will, this "giving-in" or "flowing-with" concept, can be converted to power and strength. For example, tension-relaxation, give-take, resist-yield demonstrations of alternate behavioral moods in aikido make aggression and attack futile.

In sumo, the 1500-year-old, yet modernly colorful form of Japanese wrestling, the religious roots are evident. The matches are held under a shrinelike canopy where athletes perform opening and closing ritualistic dances dedicated to the gods. Formalized costume and traditional etiquette are retained, and grand champions are honored at a great Tokyo Shinto shrine where worship is offered with a sense of awe, and outstanding persons as well as the mysteries of nature are acknowledged. For the sumo wrestler such reverence creates a sense of communion with the spirits of nature and ancestral deities. Winning is no special victory when losing is not a disgrace but rather an opportunity to lose self-importance and gain humility. Ancient sport, as practiced in modern Japan, is an art form that illustrates the philosophy of Zen.

In Buddhist-dominated Thailand many sports of Thai culture are rigorous, even barbaric, but their participants seek a quieting of the mind by preliminary meditation, acknowledgments, and ritualistic dances. Prior to cockfighting, kite combats, sword and pole fighting, and Thai's vicious style of boxing, each contestant performs a unique ritual that symbolizes respect, particularly for his trainers, and prepares him for the physical and mental challenges of encounter.

In Taiwan culture and other Sino-cultures, Tai Chi Chaun, popularly known as Chinese shadowboxing, makes a Western observer wonder what its enthusiasts are doing; such slow, exact, balletlike movements seem to be both exercise and worshipful meditation. The performers achieve, it appears, a sense of spirituality through movement; each motion exudes a feeling of peace, patience, and communion with nature. The respect for the body, the mind, and the spirit is felt as the Tai Chi is performed, whenever possible, in an early morning, outdoor setting as lovely as Taipei Park.

In the Moslem world, the Islamic prayer sequence demonstrates that "the physical embodies and expresses the spiritual."[2] Five times daily devout Muslims combine movement with meditation, as their verbal chants take them through seven steps of arm positions, forward bending, deep knee bows, and prostration positions. Afghanistani Muslims in Kabul's park often respond to the muezzin's call beside sumolike wrestling matches, which apparently are initiated spontaneously by men during their social gatherings.

In the heart of Tehran is a mosquelike sports arena, the Djafari Club, where Iranian athletes perform traditional exercises in an artistic mosaic "shrine" known as the "Gowd" or "Pit." Before entering the Gowd, athletes must purify their thoughts in a humbling attitude; even the low door to the Pit necessitates this humbling posture. Here are executed daily traditional strength exercises of "heel" (performed with giant-sized Indian clubs), stone-lifting, and kabbadeh, which is the maneuvering of a heavy bowlike metal instrument above the head. "In order to show love for the leader and to encourage patriotism, epic and narrative poems are chanted during the exercises to the beating of drums; but it is believed that the most important result of practicing traditional athletics is the mental side of it . . . and it is contended that these exercises help to raise the morale and to encourage the spirit of manhood and gallantry."[3] The Gowd is, in fact, a commemorative tomb and reminder of death, intended to divert the mind from vices and encourage bravery.[3] Athletes also pray in the "corners" of the circular pit before each activity in the event. These ancient athletics of Iran are based totally on respect, humility, generosity, and valour.[3]

"Ancient India has bequeathed to the world a veritable treasure, in fact the cream of Indian culture, in the ideology and technology of Yoga."[5] Yoga, an art and science of healthy living, suggests an integrated approach to man and treats man as a body–mind–spirit complex.[5] It is believed by the yogin that to reject the physical life is to turn away from completeness—"to ignore the body is to reject a perfect spirituality."[1] It is a goal of Yoga to ". . . establish an equilibrium between the fully active mind and the body. . . ."[1]

It has not been the purpose of this chapter to propound any religious doctrine, but to recognize the relationship of sport to spirituality, that is, life's intangible experiences, and to cite examples of sport and movement wherein man's total being may be enriched through mindful spiritual blending. And finally to raise the question: Are traditional American sports overlooking a beneficial emphasis inherent in spiritual exercise?

REFERENCES

1. Aurobindo, S.: *The Synthesis of Yoga.* Pondicherry, India: Shri Aurobindo Asham, 1971.
2. Cragg, K.: *The Call of the Minaret.* New York: Oxford University Press, 1956.
3. C. Peggy Gazette: Personal observations from visit during sabbatical year, 1973.
4. Reischauer, E. O.: *Japan: The Story of a Nation.* New York: Alfred A. Knopf Publishers, 1970.
5. Yogendra, J., and Vaz, J. C.: *Yoga Today.* Calcutta: The Macmillan Co., 1971.

SECTION III

BEING MY BODY

Chapter 11

Introduction

*I am my body. It is the embodiment of my
consciousness. My body is that by which there
are objects in my world.* *

*God guard me from the thoughts men think
In the mind alone.
He that sings a lasting song
Thinks in a marrow bone.*
> William Butler Yeats:
> *The King of the Great
> Clock Tower*

These existentially oriented reflections suggest the potential
freedom and meanings available when one "takes on" a certain
perspective of the human body, and a subsequent view of the
nature of human movement as experienced by the person in the
various sports, dance, aquatics, and other movement forms available.

Any discussion of human beings and the relationship between
mind and body is indeed problematic. The chapters in this section
consider the dimensions of the human body from cognitive,
affective, and experiential perspectives.

What is this thing called "the body"? How does it affect us as
human beings? How does it affect our world and the way we live in
it? Can we even speak of the body in this detached fashion and still
be describing the body as we actually feel it on the most basic and
primordial level of personal experience? Does the verbal explanation of the body equal the nonverbal perception we have of the
body? Is the description of the body the actuality that *is* described?
Can the explanation *be* that which is explained? Is the "word" ever
the "thing"?

Just what is the relationship between thought and action—
between mind and body? When we attempt to analyze, conceptualize, and theorize, there does indeed seem to be a division, if

*Fahey, B. W. : Basketball: A Phenomenological Perspective of Lived-Body Ex-
perience. Master's thesis. Seattle, Wash.: University of Washington, 1971.

only by the very nature of the processes of intellection. Psychologically this division seems apparent in the split or differentiation between mind and body. Is it possible that this division arises when the thinker or the experiencer is separate from that which is thought or experienced? Is there possibility for communion, for integration of this mind–body entity we call a human being. It would seem slightly less than intelligent if we conceptually attempt to make sense of the *idea of integration*—of assembling the fragments of the person to ensure a unified whole for the sake of promoting a doctrine, a formula, or a pattern in which the mind and body are one. The *idea* of integration necessarily implies someone who is an integrator and can accomplish this integration. Following this line of thought one step further, we can see that the idea or notion of integration is completely antithetical to that experiential totality which we call the person, the nonfragmented mind–body. That is, on the level of basic human experience the one who is integrating also happens to be one of the fragments (mind–body) in need of integration.

Merleau-Ponty's suggestion "I am my body" is precisely the description that presents the person and body as one. The person cannot separate self from body, because the person *is* his or her body—a whole continuous movement of intentional, embodied thought-action and a cognitive-affective-experiential process of expression.

The image we form of our body, the meaning we give it, is presented to others by the manner in which we exhibit (manifest) our body in a living situation. This is precisely the opposite of the presentation of an *idea* about the body. Generally the writers in this section focus on the person as a moving being—a psychophysiological totality of mind and body, a unified psyche-soma. They are primarily concerned with the body as an energetic process of gesture, emotion, feeling, and relationship—the body proper, the body as experienced in a lived situation.

It is suggested that to understand more clearly and to become one with the body requires a perspective which is "quiet." If we are only intellectually concerned with this idea of the integrated (mind–body) person, with the verbal and dialectical examination of the idea, we continuously run the risk of never actually being aware of what is is we are talking about, what it is we are attempting to understand. You are encouraged to read the chapters in this section with a quiet and open mind—a perspective initially free from comparison, measurement, judgment, and evaluation. Read these chapters without a sense of condemnation, a need to interpret, a desire for justification. Do not allow your past conditioning in some specialized area to filter the material presented, allowing only familiar and reinforcing information to sift through. Do not accept or deny, simply read and consider with a fresh openness new images and experiences. Free yourself from previously ingrained methodologies and systems.

Nothing is permanent about our behavior patterns except possibly our belief that they are permanent. This belief in permanence seems to occur because we take for granted that considerable time is necessary for change to occur. This is not necessarily true at all. It is only in spontaneous human action that you can prove that behavior patterns can change quickly. Let *your* body tell *you!*

Do not create any resistance from which conflict might arise. You, the thinker, create this resistance by believing that you are separate from your thoughts. On the contrary, you are your thoughts! You are your body! In assuming this perspective, you will have difficulty creating such resistance. Your body possesses its own intrinsic organic intelligence, and only a great deal of thought and observation will allow you to understand this bodily maturity or intelligence.

Moshe Feldenkrais presents a personalized view of the psychophysiological relationship between the expressive body and its gravitational functioning. He suggests that certain elements of personality and inadequate postural adjustments are related, in that some muscular adaptations (unnecessary contractions) are expressions of psychological attitudes.

Ken Ravizza presents his view of the most fundamental aspect of our human condition. He suggests that we are out of touch with our bodies and the feelings they convey. He presents some means by which we might initiate a process of engagement, leading eventually to an increase in our awareness and intensification of feeling during various movement experiences. If we can perhaps incorporate some of these suggestions into our daily living and moving patterns, we may no longer feel like "strangers in a world we never made."

Brian Fahey invites us to experience, express, and appreciate a more somatic sense of self—a personal feeling—a tone in which the body flows and pulsates in harmony with its own inner rhythms. He suggests that the dimensions of spontaneous joy and passion are authentic modes of personal existence.

Barbara Conry concludes this section on bodily dimensions with a precise phenomenological account of a meditative experience through yoga. As in the previous writings in this section, the emphasis is on the importance of the person as a subjective being. She suggests that on completion of a series of reductions one might have access to an experience of oneself as a pure embodied consciousness who is both creator and experiencer of one's life-world.

Chapter 12

Motility and Adjustment*

Moshe Feldenkrais

All movement, whatever its purpose may be, like closing the eyes when remembering or thinking, is, in the last analysis, an antigravity action. Not only is the ocular globe moved as a mass in the field of gravitation, but the rest of the body is set in a special attitude and is thus maintained against the tendency of gravitation to bring it down. There is little awareness of all this constant adjustment to very stringent requirements, but the nervous system is constantly and without break, responsive to gravitation, so long as there is any life in it. Therefore, when we speak of antigravity function, we refer to motility in general.

The importance of the gravitation function, anatomically and from a mechanical point of view, has been raised in our exposition to such pre-eminence that one would expect very serious consequences in all cases where the adaptation to gravity is not perfect. Yet not only only are persons with perfect body mechanics rare, but we often see individuals with very poor body mechanisms apparently successful and content.

The situation is similar to that shown by psychoanalysis. Here, too, persons with perfect libido history and development are rare, yet we see many apparently happy individuals afflicted with all sorts of complexes.

There are two main reasons for this apparent discrepancy between theory and practice.

(a) The unique freedom in man for making personal muscular patterns for all acts.
(b) Tradition and habit.

The act of sitting, for instance, may be learned to become so conditioned to the chair that the Japanese and Bedouin modes of sitting without the use of appliances or furniture become impossible altogether. I know an example of a well-known scientist who could not sit in the Japanese style after four years' repeated trials twice a week. And this in spite of the fact that in early childhood children so sit quite spontaneously in the same fashion all over the world without any sitting implement.

The unique facility of learning in man is responsible not only for the great divergence of manner in the most elementary acts, unknown in any other species, even among individuals of different continents, but it also explains how it is possible to do and think quite improperly and yet feel right. There being no instinctive mode of doing in most acts, we can learn any performance. The improper mode, however, needs conscious attention and has always elements of indirectness in it; the "roundabout" approach to the simplest problem is the outstanding feature of inferior learning. Such learning tends to reinstate situations in their minutest details which acquire an exaggerated importance, often greater than the act itself. In habitual acts and situations, it is always possible to learn to achieve a goal, no matter how unsatisfactory the mode of doing may be from a more general point of view; one has time to think and get ready, also, habitual circumstances are rarely of crucial importance, so that no immediate bad consequences are noticeable. In suddenly changing conditions, the fault becomes glaringly obvious, just as emotional maladjustment shows up in sharp traumatic events.

The second reason is mainly founded on ignorance. Most people are prone to find faults in their body and behaviour, but do not know what to do about correcting the situation. Later, when grown up, most people give up the idea of basic change in themselves. The idea that faulty behaviour is a personal misfortune often leads to the conclusion that it must be covered up. The result is that the majority present outwardly a veneer designed to cover up all shortcomings.

From early childhood, they receive confirmation that this is the right thing to do. They see their parents changing their comportment, dress and general behaviour when they go out. They see their teachers do the same thing when a person of authority visits the school. They are actually given guidance to learn this covering up of inadequate posture and behaviour, instead of being helped to learn the proper way.

There are some fortunate children who are given constructive guidance, or are left alone; the majority, however, receive instruction of an affective character only. It is "do" or "don't" with no guidance how to comply with these instructions. More often than not, the child is already aware of what is wanted, but cannot do it. It is wrong to order a child to sit up. If he does not do so himself, he has already been thrown out of proper development, and something must be done to make him feel right only in the proper posture. Goading or punishment only distort the emotional pattern, and force the child to cover up the symptom which is the cause of his troubles. He is not improving, but hiding his faults. He soon learns to put on a suit of character when not alone to hide the real self.

Most people actually change their habitual posture on leaving home, when being observed or when unexpectedly confronted with a person whose relation to them is of interest. Obviously, they are aware of their normal inadequacy. Everybody works out his personal pattern of holding breath, of stiffening here and there— smartening up, it is called—contracting his mouth or brows; in fact, every part of his body that he believes may convey an idea of his personality. This method of covering up instead of perfecting, being the result of ignorance, succeeds only superficially. Even though ingenious persons may develop this masquerade business to an astonishing degree of perfection, and waste real gifts on futile procedure, they sooner or later come to feel a sense of emptiness and futility, and many lose interest in life.

The neurotic achieves an outward appearance of well-being by a consciously adopted presentation of himself which, however, rarely misleads the specialist's eye. The inadequate adjustment to gravity is also masked in the same way, but it is much more difficult to disguise this inadequacy than any other. For the veneer consists of a conscious muscular effort supplementing the usual one. This is always directly noticeable, especially if the subject is unaware that he is observed. It is particularly evident at all times of sudden disturbances. The veneer put on to make oneself "presentable" is too transparent to cover up improper antigravity adjustment; but it is necessary to know what to look for. The person with inadequate antigravity adjustment excludes certain attitudes more or less totally according to the seriousness of his case.

We are generally concerned with what a person does or has achieved, rather than how he does it. On shifting our attention to examine the quality of the act, the ease, the time necessary to initiate an act, the amount of interference a person can stand before the act is upset—in short, if we examine the manner instead of the result of doing, the inadequate adjustment shows up much more readily.

We have seen previously that to eliminate the capacity of locomotion completely, nothing short of total destruction will do.

Without legs, even without limbs altogether, moving along is still possible. If we look at what is achieved without concern as to how it is achieved, we could hardly tell a legless person from a normal one; both may have moved from the place in which we left them to the new place where we now observe them. Only because the way in which they achieve the displacement is so different, is the difference between two such persons so outstanding. In acts where the mechanisms at work are not readily observable, it is difficult to tell a cripple from a normal person just by examining the final result. We consider two fathers. The psychiatrist with more intimate knowledge may find one a normal person and the other a total wreck. When we are able to gain more intimate knowledge of how people achieved the immediately apparent success, we find so much misery behind the bright spots put out to be seen, that many feel rather inclined to pity humanity as a whole.

Anyone who has been able to give some sort of help, or even only hope, to bring about improvement, can tell of continuous surprise to find among his callers people whom, in his ignorance, he always considered as outstanding successes. He soon gets used to it, and is not astonished to find first-rate athletes complaining of premature ejaculation, successful dynamic financiers complaining of lack of interest in life, brilliant scientists who cannot manage the experiment of marital life, painters who cannot love, actors who stammer, etc.

We may conclude that the serious consequences of improper adjustment to gravity are veiled in the same way as improper development of the libido, or social adjustment, or any adaptation for that matter.

It is obvious that in order to get some sense out of this complex question it is necessary to have a clear idea of what is proper or correct in human behaviour. There is usually a moral code inherited from religious practice or social justice and convenience lying behind all our activity. In general, the average behaviour is the standard of good or fitting behaviour. This is a low minimum indeed, far below the potential capacity of most of us. In modern society specialisation is an absolute necessity. Obviously then, some of our potentialities must be in relative abeyance. My contention is that in properly mature persons no faculty and no articulation is so utterly excluded from use directly or indirectly as to render it unserviceable.

Man's capacity to make personal nervous and muscular patterns was associated with the fact that innervations concerned with voluntary movements grow while the control of action is being learned. All the new responses he acquires are integrated into a vast background of vegetative and reflex activity. He learns to speak, to walk, to adjust himself to his parents, and to other members of his society all at once. Concurrently, the libido shapes itself from primitive, diffuse, erotic urges, shifting from one object to another until it reaches a final stage of mature heterosexual character. All these different patterns developing simultaneously, are interwoven not only on the mental plane, but also in the body. To every attitude there corresponds not only an affective state, but a muscular pattern of the face as well as of all muscles in general.

We can therefore analyse the course of development of a personality by fixing our attention on one of these adjustments. Each of them may be chosen as representative of the individuality under examination. All of them have the disadvantage of depending upon and involving the subject himself in the procedure of his own analysis. In all, the vehicle by which the analysis is performed, is speech. This is, for the majority of people, a very clumsy means of conveying precise information. The same words often mean quite different things to different persons. To describe a movement or an event that can be seen in a fraction of a second, a cumbersome flow of words is necessary. Even then there is little precision in the description, and expressions like "you know what I mean" crop up sooner or later. Any visual and tactile evidence must therefore be considered as more reliable, as well as labour saving.

Taking this viewpoint with regard to the ground we have covered, it is quite obvious that the most suitable function for analysing the development of a personality is his muscular activity. The closer one looks into the problem, the clearer it becomes that this is correct. For instance, it is desirable to define clearly and precisely what constitutes proper behaviour. Well, what is a proper libido development or a proper adjustment to society? It is hard to believe, yet it is a fact, that although the libido is the central problem of psychoanalysis, there is no clear and precise description of a proper sexual act, in all the classical literature on the subject. Because of correlation, however, the general trend of development can be studied in any function. Maturity of the antigravity function is apparent in the erect potent posture. It is much easier to define the potential erect posture, and we shall see in precise mechanical terms of what it consists.

It seems correct to think that all hindrance in the development of the libido will be noticeable primarily in the sexual act itself, and not only in secondary and auxiliary manifestations of the sexual instinct. If the average man's behaviour is neurotic, the sexual act of the average man is not what it might be potentially. By the principle of correlation, all adaptations and adjustments should bear the same general character. Maladjustment in respect of any adaptation should be, and is, observable in the antigravity function as well. It is known, in fact, from observation, that neurotic persons present peculiarities in the antigravity muscles. To cite Professor Josephine Rathbone:[1] ". . . it is quite safe to suggest one empirical hypothesis, which has grown out of observation of individuals who are having serious emotional difficulties. It appears that many of them lose the ability to stand in complete extension, and assume a position of more or less flexion."

How does this come about?

Erect posture, for which the human body is best suited, is essentially such that little effort is required in maintaining it; standing is a higher performance than advancing. Improper standing is arrested or incompleted learning. Moreover, greater muscular effort is necessary in standing without complete extension. As in all improperly performed acts, greater energy expenditure is involved in the case of improper standing. We have, however, seen that exteroceptive, proprioceptive, otolithic, and labyrinthine reflexes are responsible for the posture of animals. In man, we said that the optical righting and the conscious function have an overriding influence, and that all the impulses are algebraically added to produce the result. Two alternatives could account for a person continuously maintaining a posture different from the one the reflex mechanisms are best fitted for. First, faulty mechanisms, either inherited or diseased. There are certainly such cases, but they give trouble from earliest infancy. Second, the conscious overriding control, all the elements of which are acquired through personal experience, is responsible for the faulty activity. In most cases anatomical lesion is excluded, and we conclude that the overriding control gives directions contradicting the other reflex impulses from all the gravity-concerned centres. If this is the case, there must be muscular contraction present that is not indispensable for maintaining the proper erect posture. Unnecessary muscular contraction is, in fact, easy to demonstrate in all cases of improper posture. Close study shows that we deal with faulty distribution of activity, i.e., some muscular groups are doing unnecessary work while others are flabby and toneless.

Every function has its own vulnerable points, where most faults are likely to occur. In psychoanalysis we know of Oedipus complex, castration complex, and the like. These occur at crucial periods of development of the libido. And if the learning process is halted there, a clear case is present.

The adjustment to gravity has its own history with similar foci of arrested development. The spine, in early childhood, is practically straight, and the cervical curve begins to form before the lumbar curvature. Thus the shoulder, neck and sacro-lumbar regions are those in which most incomplete, or otherwise faulty, learning will find its halting barrier. These are mechanically the regions in which the greatest muscular adjustment is necessary, because very heavy masses have to be properly aligned with great precision. Also many of the muscles of these regions act on more than one joint, and their control is more delicate. Moreover, twisting of the body around the vertical axis, through the centre of gravity, for which the human frame is predominantly fitted, and which is a special advantage of the human erect posture, takes place mainly in these two regions.

With the head prevented from turning right and left on its support, and lumbar vertebrae made rigid too, turning of the body becomes an awkward, laborious, and slow operation, necessitating at least three steps. We have seen in reviewing Magnus's work that these two regions play, in fact, a unique part in the antigravity muscular adjustment. They may be considered as a kind of sense organ. The neck and pelvis tonic standing and righting reflexes are initiated in the muscles of these regions.

If the conscious control or the optical righting reflexes are responsible for faulty posture, then their elimination should leave the lower centres in control, and a reduction of flexion should take place, and the carriage should become more erect. Under hypnotism and spontaneous somnambulic states, the head is, in fact, lifted and the pelvis straightened, so that the person stands taller than in his normal waking state. Blind people, too, carry their head higher than the average. Thus, if an actor is to play the part of a blind man on the stage, it is enough for him to raise and immobilise the head in its rotation around the vertical axis, i.e., to turn the whole trunk with the head rigid but upright, to find the audience at once comprehending the situation.

In short, arrested development leaves its mark on all the functions without exception. Digestion, breathing, muscular control, sexual act, and social adjustment are all affected simultaneously. Only deep emotional disturbances can so affect the conscious control as to distort the appreciation of the environment, and yet leave the subject in ignorance to continue in an imaginary world of his own.

REFERENCE

1. *Corrective Physical Education* (Saunders), 2nd Edition, page 106.

chapter 13

The Body Unaware

Kenneth Ravizza

I am a stranger and afraid in a world I never made.
—A. E. Housman

As A. E. Housman observed, tremendous technological advances have induced in man a tragic sense of fear and alienation from his environment. Specialization, complexity, and the transient nature of things have made it difficult for man to feel at home in his world. The pervading economic, social, ecological, and population dilemmas are so vast that many persons are bewildered by them. They feel a sense of helplessness which produces an overwhelming apathy and a desire to avoid the problems confronting them. One method of avoidance is explained by Erich Fromm: "... to give up the independence of one's own self and to fuse one's self with somebody or something outside of oneself in order to acquire the strength which the individual self is lacking."[4] Overcome by helplessness and unable to cope, individuals reach out for some external force to solve their problem. Thus, there are disillusioned persons who simply ignore the manifold problems associated with today's progressive and complex technology. Others, when confronted with personal and/or physical problems, seek solutions that merely gloss over the underlying cause.

The confused state of affairs is revealed in the many individuals who are out of touch with their own bodies. In an attempt to deal with technological developments, man has developed his mental and conceptual capacities, but he has neglected his direct bodily experiences and sensations. R. D. Laing addressed this problem when he stated:

> As adults, we have forgotten most of our childhood, not only its contents but its flavor; as men of the world, we hardly know of the existence of the inner world ... or for our bodies, we retain just sufficient proprioceptive sensations to co-ordinate our movements and to ensure the minimal requirements for biosocial survival—beyond that, little or nothing.[3]

Individuals do not manifest an awareness of their inner world of direct firsthand experience and the body awareness that contributes to an understanding of it. As Laing points out, persons are aware only to a minimal degree, recognizing when the body is not feeling "normal," and adopting some external remedy to resolve the problem.

Confronted with a physical ailment, some persons reach for a pharmaceutical product as an instant remedy. Reliance on external products for relief is overwhelming: pills to go to sleep, pills to stay awake, pills for diets, pills for tensions, and pills for depression. "Five thousand million pills a year" are swallowed in the United States alone in order for individuals to cope with their problems.[2] Seldom do persons attempt to confront the possible cause and assume the responsibility of working through their problems, whether tension, anxiety, tiredness, overweight. Aspirin does nothing for the actual source of the pain, but it does deaden one's awareness of the pain.

The nonchalant attitude of relief being only a swallow away has caused individuals gradually to become dependent on external stimuli to remedy their problems. Neglect of body awareness is also reflected in man's slavery to the clock. Some check the time to discover if they are hungry, sleepy, and the like, according to the appropriate hour of the day. This indicates the widespread unawareness they have of their natural body rhythms.

Reliance on externals reflects the attitude which regards the body as a mechanism that the individual must keep tuned in order to transport him. Rollo May expounded:

> As a result of ... suppressing the body into an inanimate machine, subordinated to the purpose of modern industrialism, people are proud of paying no attention to the body. They treat it as an object for manipulation, as though it were a truck to be driven till it runs out of gas.... They know how germs or virus or allergies attack the body, and they also know how penicillin or sulfa or some other drug cures them. The attitude toward disease is not that of the self-aware person who experiences his body as part of himself....[9]

Physical educators have unintentionally contributed to the conception of the body as an animated machine; viewing it primarily as an object of scientific analysis. In the minds of the public, physical education is associated chiefly with physical fitness—the physical educator is the person who gets one's body in good physical condition, just as the dentist gets one's teeth in order. He spends time and energy measuring persons before, during, and after participating in his programs to determine their level of fitness.

Of course, the elaborate body-conditioning programs used in this conditioning of the animated machines do produce results. When students finish the program, they are usually in significantly better shape. But the statistics do not reveal what the students' physical condition is six months after they have completed the program. Often, persons enroll in physical fitness classes anticipating that the instructor will furnish the motivation for them to work at their maximum. Once the course is completed and the "motivator" is removed, they often regress to their previous out-of-shape state, and the trim new silhouette soon sags. The instructor's interest is ephemeral, and the student must be prepared to continue the program on his own. In most conditioning programs, the primary goal is to work the student into good shape. But, when do most persons who work out feel good? Usually, an individual feels best when the day's exercise is completed. It is as though the workout itself is an arduous battle and the victory comes when the battle ends. It is synonymous with the story of the moron who enjoys banging his head against the wall because it feels good when he stops. When the instructor becomes the significant motivating force, it merely reflects another instance when the individual is motivated by an external force.

Physical educators tend to objectify the body, not only in relation to physical fitness but also in the areas of kinesiology, biomechanics, and motor learning. As a result, individuals are conditioned to relate to the body as an object outside of themselves to be "whipped into shape" or disciplined in learning motor skills. Unknowingly, physical educators encourage the participant to view himself as a duality—a mind and a body. This is confusing because man does not live his existence as separate parts, but as a total functioning being. Sy Kleinman addressed this point when he wrote:

> We have come to regard the body as a thing to be dealt
> with rather than as an existent presence or mode of
> being. . . . We have divorced the body from experience
> and we do not attempt to understand it as it operates
> in the lived world. Rather, we attempt to explain it as

a physiological organism. We don't look at it as it is,
but as we conceptualize it scientifically.[7]

It is the concept that persons are totally functioning human beings and not just physical bodies in the physical education class that I wish to develop. Because many individuals relate to the body as an object, it is difficult to have them become aware of the signals the body is constantly receiving from the external environment. Bodily signals are ever-present, for example, in the contracting of the shoulders in a tense or stressful encounter with someone. Severin Peterson stated: "The less the body is experienced, the more it becomes an appearance; the less reality it has, the more it must be undressed or dressed up; the less it is one's own known body, the further away it moves from anything to do with one's self." It is the conception of the body as an object outside and separate from the self that must be changed.

Although it may be difficult to increase a person's awareness after he has neglected it for so long, a multitude of insights can be gained from daily occurrences, if one is willing to focus attention on bodily experiences. One hindrance is our preoccupation with getting somewhere, we often overlook what is happening to the body directly during the journey. Usually, we begin our day relaxed, but as the day progresses, we confront a variety of stressful situations which gradually result in a tightening of the muscles as this tension is channeled into the body. The body reveals tension through a sore neck, a backache, tight shoulders, and a wrinkled, contorted face.

Another problem confronting the individual who is attempting to develop an awareness of his body is that as man developed his cognitive abilities he began to overlook the significance of firsthand experiences, dealing instead with abstract concepts of direct experiences. It appears that man shifted his attention from living the experience to conceptualizing about the experience. Rollo May stated:

> *Many disturbances of bodily functions, beginning in*
> *such simple things as incorrect walking, or faulty*
> *posture or breathing, are due to the fact that people*
> *have all their lives walked, to take only one simple*
> *illustration, as though they were machines, and have*
> *never experienced any of the feelings in their feet or*
> *legs or rest of the body.*[9]

It is lack of awareness of the body that contributes to a multitude of postural and lower back problems that plague millions of middle-aged Americans. Are you aware of how you are sitting as you read this article? Is your spine slouched over the paper? Are your shoulders rounded? Do you want to be in such a tight posture? What is it doing to your body? It is interesting to note that whenever a malfunction of an extremity is corrected (e.g., by knee operation), the patient must consciously feel what it is like to walk again. It is necessary for the patient to focus total attention on the extremity and to attempt to feel what it is like to use it properly.

The emphasis that society places on achieving goals is reflected in an individual's neglect of his body. He lacks an awareness of "process" because so often he holds preestablished conceptions, values, and opinions that the process is painful, or at least uncomfortable. But awareness is hidden in the process and for this reason the person must attempt to focus directly on it.

An example of a process slighted in movement is the common presupposition that jogging is ugly; this may be a valid opinion, especially if the individual experienced or observed jogging being used as punishment in his physical education class. The person has a negative conception of jogging and this accompanies the experience. However, if the individual is encouraged to suspend this negative connotation temporarily and slowly jog at a comfortable pace and to focus his attention on the process (for example, the flow of energy through the body, bodily sensations, personal feelings, and the like) a new positive jogging experience could occur.

The individual may begin to experience jogging as more than just physical conditioning and a painful experience. He may use it as an opportunity to focus his attention and become aware of the strength, endurance, natural rhythm, and flowing qualities that he possesses as a moving being. Instead of running to get somewhere and constantly attempting to ignore the process, the individual can look at the experience as beneficial and not only at the long-range effect of jogging. By removing the negative connotations surrounding the process, it would make the actual jogging more enjoyable and he would be more apt to continue.

Another way to develop an awareness of process is to encourage a student to adopt temporarily a different perspective on the activity. In football, a defensive end could gain insights into his position if he could view his position from the offensive end's perspective. By discussing his perception of the opposing player,

the defensive end may be better able to visualize his own task and
its relation to the total team effort. Athletes could suspend some of
their set ways expressly to allow them to observe and become
aware of diverse aspects of their participation that were previously
unnoticed. When a player's only concern is the final outcome, he
loses many pertinent new insights and discoveries inherent in the
process.

Awareness of the body is an integral aspect of the process of
life. Alexander Lowen addressed this when he stated:

> *Self-awareness is a function of feeling. It is the
> summation of all body sensations at any one time.
> Through his self-awareness a person knows who he is.
> He is aware of what is going on in every part of his
> body; in other words, he is in touch with himself. For
> example, he senses the flow of feeling in his body
> associated with breathing, and senses all other
> spontaneous or involuntary body movements. But he
> is also aware of the muscular tensions that restrict his
> movements, for these too create sensations. . . . Not
> being in touch with his body from within, it feels
> strange and awkward to him, which makes him feel
> self-conscious in his expression and movement.*[8]

One may develop an awareness of body by becoming totally
involved in what one is doing. So often in the classroom, students
are not totally "there"; their bodies are seated in the proper
location, but their minds are wandering—thinking of a tough
practice session that afternoon or a big party the next weekend.
Maybe as you read this article you find mind wandering? Where are
you?

Integrating mind and body so as to focus on what is happening
in the present increases one's awareness; the experience is intensi-
fied as a result of full attention being given to the experience. One
can view the experience as if one was focusing a camera. The individual is zoomed right into what is happening. Eleanor Criswell
discussed this different kind of concentration.

> *The first thing you have to do is to learn the trick of
> undivided attention or concentration. By these terms,
> I mean something quite different from what is
> ordinarily meant. One "concentrates" on writing a
> chapter in a book, or on solving problem in mathe-*

> *matics; but this is a complicated process of dividing one's attention, giving it to one detail after another, judging, balancing, making decisions. The kind of concentration I mean is putting the attention on one object, or one uncomplicated thought, such as joy, or peace, and holding it there steadily. It isn't thinking; it is inhibiting thought, except for one thought, or one object of thought.* [1]

It is this type of concentration that can be used in becoming aware of one's body while moving. To direct this type of concentration one's bodily experience definitely intensifies the experience. As stated, one can begin to do this by bringing mind and body together to focus on the present or "now" moment phenomenon. One of the first and most important lessons I learned in hatha yoga was that an attempt is made to bring a previously unnoticed awareness to the exercise. As revealed in toe touching, one coordinates mind, body, and breath. Breath is used because it aids the mover in focusing on the present movement; breath can also be used to direct the movement by inhaling with exertion and exhaling and letting go. Breath is a pertinent quality of the moving being and it contributes to moving as total being.

One begins toe touching by changing the temporal aspect and slowing down the exercise so that one can concentrate on the total body stretch and not merely count the number of stretches left to do. Stretch is not limited to the legs, for a person can carry that feeling of stretch into the lower back where so much tension is held; he can stretch the spinal column as he extends forward; he can even carry or direct this stretch all the way to the neck area. As the individual slowly stretches, he reaches a point where there is a slight pain; he can then work breathing with the stretch and *consciously think* of letting go of the tightness at each exhalation. Not only will this ease any discomfort, but it will also enable the person to stretch past that painful point and consciously be aware of the physical release.

Slowing down movement may also be utilized in the skill class to aid students in the development of the basic skill techniques. The assumption is that, if the movement is slowed down, the student will be able to focus in on his awareness of the movement. One college student commented on this slow-motion technique in learning to dribble a soccer ball: "There was so much more time to think, change your mind about how to stroke the ball before you actually had to . . . I had to pay attention to my feelings more."

Another technique that may be used to develop a student's concentration is to alter his sense perspective so that he is forced to take a new "outlook." This may be done by "closing off" various senses. While working with beginning wrestlers, I found it beneficial to use blindfolds on the wrestlers to aid them in developing the bodily feel for when to execute certain moves. The wrestler has to become more aware of his body because he cannot see. Clearly, a great deal of exploration, creativity, and experimentation is possible and needed in this realm.

The technique of focusing attention on the present and bringing mind and body together will enable the athlete to concentrate on an awareness of his body. This concentration is common in athletics as evidenced by the psyching-up process. The athlete often prepares for a game by narrowing his thought process on the immediate contest. He dismisses all thoughts that are irrelevant to the actual playing of the game. His concentration is intense and centered only on the game. The player is not consciously thinking about what he is doing, he is just doing it.

When a player has his basic skills under control, he begins to react spontaneously to the situation as it presents itself. He does not have time to think things out, instead he experiences the event directly. At the beginning of a game, there is a period when the player attempts to pick up the tempo of the game. A player does not conceptualize and categorize this, but experiences and feels it directly. He knows what the tempo of the game is by being part of it.

Another technique one can use to develop awareness is to develop a feeling of being "centered," then move and experience from this center. A centered position is a balanced, stable position. The person moves, directs his energy, gives, and flows with the experience from this place. By exploring his inner space, he may locate this center. Charlotte Selver explains how one can find this center by becoming aware of one's position in standing.

> *Standing is the starting point of greatest potential for physical activity, from which walking, running, fighting, dancing and all sports begin and to which they return. It is the specifically human activity, which is exploited by all the less civilized people and by children who have not yet abandoned its uses and pleasures for the chimera of "relaxation." Easy and balanced standing, in which our inner reactiveness mobilizes precisely the energy needed to counter-*

balance the pull of earth, permits a full sensing of the total organism.[1]

By moving from the center one gathers oneself within and moves from this space. The person moves to the outside from a place of strength and not merely from a diffused position within. The natural athlete is the player who unconsciously moves from this place; it is natural for him and may explain why he can adjust to so many sport movements. The centered position grounds our awareness, and it is from here that we can tell when we are off balance or some part of our body is tense and needs attention.

The centered position can be developed by having the student unbalance himself to the right or left, front or back. He can also become aware of the centered position by stretching various muscles and then contracting them and observing where the center is when they return to normal position. For example, pull your eyebrows out to the side and notice where they are when they return. That spot is a centered position for the eyebrows. There is a centered position in the body, but as we tense and contort it throughout the day we become uptight and often lop-sided and off center.

It is important to learn centered position, for it will enable us to live and experience the body from a constant space. In a world that is ever-changing, a constant space within ourselves may become like a safe harbor to a battered ship.

In summary, one can develop an awareness of body by first suspending personal values and viewing participation in sport or movement from another perspective. An integration of mind and body also contributes to this development, for the person is more involved in what is happening to him directly. Moving from a centered position with one's awareness focused on what is happening at the present moment is the final way awareness may be increased.

Many of the examples given in this chapter are related to participation in sport, but physical educators have other students who are in dire need of developing their awarenesses and sensitivities so that they can better cope with the pressures and tensions of today's world.

By becoming aware of body, individuals can learn to conserve energy and use only the energy necessary to complete a task. This conservation would eliminate the energy wasted by constant overexertion. If this energy can be saved, it may reduce the exhaustion experienced at the end of the day. For example, how much strength do you need to pick up a piece of paper? How much do you use? How much energy do you waste lifting improperly?

Second, if an awareness of the body is developed, we can become aware of tension and deal with it immediately. So often we just hold this tension in and exist from a tense perspective until we reach the gymnasium and physically work off this tension. There is no reason why we cannot deal with the tension right at the moment and release it by stretching and letting it go. Is there a rule stating one can only exercise and get release in a gymnasium? Hugh Prather stated:

> *For several months now I have been stretching whatever wants to be stretched, making up how I do it as I go along, letting my muscles and joints tell me what they need, doing it whenever and for as long as it feels good. The effect, especially as compared to routine body-tightening calisthenics, is so mentally releasing that I believe it somehow nourishes my psyche, just as eating exactly what my stomach tells me it wants nourishes my flesh.*[11]

A practical application of this technique is dealing with headaches. If one can "catch" a headache once it starts and work at releasing the underlying tension, one need not wait until the pain builds up and a pill is the only means of combating it. Another example of this letting go is discussed by Graf von Durckheim in relation to relaxation.

> *We need to learn to relax ourselves—not only our bodies—in the right way. This entails far more than a relaxation of the muscles. Dropping the shoulders and letting go of one's self in the dropping of the shoulders are two fundamentally different movements.*[5]

This is a distinction between merely physically letting go and totally letting go. Graf von Durckheim is not concerned with just the relaxing of the body; he is an advocator of the total integrated person letting go and releasing the pent tension, releasing the psychological, social, and other pressures that often accompany tension. This is what he means by "letting go of one's self in the dropping of the shoulders."

When an individual is fully aware of the body, immediately

adjusting to the tension and messages that rise from within, he is not fighting himself; he is not holding in great amounts of tension. Instead, he is open, living in the present, integrated, and flowing directly with his experiences. Indeed, he is better prepared to deal with the pressures and forces at play in our technological world so that he need not feel as Housman expressed: "I am a stranger and afraid, in a world I never made."[6]

REFERENCES

1. Anderson, M., and Savory, L.: *Passages: A Guide for Pilgrims of the Mind.* New York: Harper & Row Publishers, 1972.
2. Blythe, P.: *Stress Disease: The Emotional Plague.* New York: St. Martins Press, 1973.
3. Christian, J.: *Philosophy: An Introduction to the Art of Wondering.* San Francisco: Rinehart Press, 1973.
4. Fromm, E.: *Escape from Freedom.* New York: Holt, Rinehart and Winston Inc., 1941.
5. Graf von Durckheim, K.: *Daily Life as Spiritual Exercise.* New York: Harper & Row, 1971.
6. Housman, A. E.: *Complete Poems.* New York: Henry Holt and Co., 1959.
7. Kleinman, S.: The significance of human movement: A phenomenological approach. In *Sport and The Body.* Edited by E. W. Gerber. Philadelphia: Lea & Febiger, 1972.
8. Lowen, A.: *Pleasure.* New York: Lancer Books, 1970.
9. May, R.: *Man's Search for Himself.* New York: The New American Library, 1967.
10. Peterson, S. (Ed.) *A Catalog of the Ways People Grow.* New York: Ballantine Books, 1971.
11. Prather, H.: *I Touch The Earth, The Earth Touches Me.* New York: Doubleday and Co. Inc., 1972.

Chapter 14

The Passionate Body

Brian W. Fahey

The purpose of this chapter is to share with you the experiential components of a particular mode of bodily being that others and I have experienced while participating in sport, athletics, dance, and other forms of physical activity. Such a task really involves a sharing and relating of one's inwardness. On a most personal level this inward feeling often lacks a sense of logical consistency and I infrequently catch glimpses of this mode of bodily being during spontaneous moments of joy and passion, interspersed with sadness and pain. It seems to be grounded in an inner sense of passion, a particular kind of experiential ecstasy that I feel when I am one with my body.

Sometimes while participating in a movement activity you may have had the feeling that everything was right, everything was occurring as it should—naturally, perfectly, effortlessly. Your actions were totally free and spontaneous, yet you felt calmly in control. You were operating from that calm place within yourself with perfect balance and harmony. You were centered! We have all had times when "it" just happened. This "it" may have been that perfect wave while surfing, the effortless run of the day while skiing, the best shots in basketball that were going to go in no matter what, or perhaps it was just you alone, running through your favorite space in that noncompetitive perfect run of joy when your breath just kept rolling in and out and you felt as though you could have run forever.

It is my belief that these "states of consciousness" and others like them take place when you are centered and your sense of self is characterized by an inner sense of passionate appreciation for the unique insights that you can discover from the body.

From this perspective, passion is viewed as an organismic state which enhances one's energy level to such an extent that one is charged and renewed with the qualitative taste of a life-state which pulsates and continues to give one a sense of what is possible. This sense of passion can be likened to a feeling-tone in which the power and sweetness of the body, the incarnate flesh, are allowed to flow, expressing a receptive quality in all of the body's movements.

I suggest that only those who can honestly identify with and feel secure in their bodies have access to the dimensions of spontaneous joy and passion. Such a state becomes possible when we permit ourselves to be aware of our own joy in the process of releasing joy and affirming the basic integrity of the body.

It is my position that the natural condition of the human organism is joy and authentic pleasure in the moment; whereas the present social system with its emphasis on rationality, control, and standardized response is unnatural. In this state of joy and passion the moving body seems to dance as the person realizes how good it feels to cooperate with instinctual nature.

Instinctive movement can be likened to a nonverbal mode of regaining balance and experiencing unity in life. In the process of moving in accordance with the natural flow of one's organism, one spontaneously senses a unique emergence of self. One is alive when and because one moves, but totally alive only when the movements are spontaneous, vital, alive, and free rather than frozen, immobile, and unresponsive.

In order to achieve this natural state, one must be receptive to bodily change in order to receive clear messages and set the stage for a re-experience of oneself as a unique totality. If one continues to regard the body as an objective entity, this psychosomatic unity cannot be realized.

An acceptance of basic bodily feelings within the boundaries of one's existence is the initial step toward understanding and desiring bodily integration. This experience is a prerequisite for understanding the experience of joy in movement. The essence of what we are seeking is an experiential flow of bodily pleasure and joy. Spontaneous movement in living one's daily existence is basic to this experience and can be compared to a subconscious acting out or movement toward passion, a striving for pleasure through regulating bodily processes and enjoying the potential release it affords. This will assist in keeping the organism in a positive (non-static) life-state.

In many instances, the exercise and experience of spontaneous feeling are subordinated to the value priorities of the empirical ego. By repressing spontaneous emotion, self-created tension blocks the natural flow of body energy, often resulting in a diminished energy metabolism and a subsequent loss of feeling-tone throughout the entire body. This can be understood as a reduction in the aliveness and potential responsiveness that normally characterize the "passionate body." Spontaneous movement can allow an individual to have an inwardly encouraged opportunity to express a positive identification with the body and the subsequent pleasure and joy experienced in its spontaneous functioning. This would occur normally as an afterthought during honest reflection upon the nature of one's human condition.

The level of pleasure is in close alignment with the level of maturity of the rhythmic bodily processes. The more spontaneous and rhythmic (natural) the motoric functions of our body, the greater the capacity for pleasurable movement experiences. Spontaneous movement is pleasureful movement and is oriented toward psychological growth. Other, more regulated and constrained movements may have pleasureful elements but they are not usually growth-oriented. Rather, they are maintenance-oriented because they deny the natural life-cycle processes with their primordial base in spontaneity. Pleasure is more than discharge of tension or satisfaction of ego-needs. With a self-created mind-body conflict present, the realization and acknowledgment of needs become diminished or blocked to such an extent that the lack of bodily fulfillment is not experienced as such. The level of the experience of well-being is such that the basic integrity and organic intelligence of the body are denied by being so strongly under ego-control. This state is not growth-oriented because it makes evaluations on the basis of *maintaining* and not *improving* the physical integrity of the organism. Actualized pleasure is expressive of organismic growth which goes beyond a mere maintenance of bodily status quo.

The capacity for pleasure is closely related to a person's level of activation (readiness) and need for excitation. The authentic dimension of this state of excitation is not an anxious longing but is existential in nature. It does not possess the utilitarian component of a longing for personal consumption and gratification. It is a letting be, an opening up, and a letting out, instead of a taking in, consumptive orientation. It is a here-and-now process.

The body cannot be viewed as a closed system. It is an on-going process interacting with the flow of its environment. Its natural movements are spontaneous and constitute the language of the ego-less body. (This should not be confused with the better known concept of "body language," the movements of which are primarily ego-dominated.) Authentic involvement in sport and other movement forms offers human beings an opportunity to re-engage in rhythmic,* qualitative movements which may have been denied them in many of their daily activities.

Mobility serves as the physiological basis for a pleasure principle which is dependent on the person's ability (state of readiness) and willingness to experience and express the spontaneous movements of the living body. The body and not the ego is subsequently realized (experienced on its most fundamental level). As Alexander Lowen suggests:

> *As long as the body remains an object of the ego, it may fulfill the ego's pride but it will never provide the joy and satisfaction that the alive body offers.*

> *The alive body is characterized by a life of its own. It has a mobility independent of ego control which is manifested by the spontaneity of its gestures and the vivacity of its expression. It hums, it vibrates, it glows. It is charged with feeling.*[3]

In order to examine more closely the relationships between ego-controlled body movement and spontaneous body movement, I would like to compare them to Lowen's discussion of mature and immature orgasm.

Mature orgasm is process-centered, ego-less, involuntary, experientially oriented; it involves the whole body as an integrated unit and its movements are flowing and spontaneous. Immature (incomplete) orgasm is product-centered and its movements are voluntary and under ego-control. It is technique-oriented, with compulsive and rigid movements. It is partial because the ego exists as something apart from (a spectator of) the movements of the body. In mature orgasm, the person shares in the kinesthetic sensation of the involuntary movements by allowing the whole body to feel the excitation of the movements. This involves giving oneself over (letting go) to the excitement and joy of moving and feeling; in a sense the body moves the ego. In immature orgasm, the ego directs the proceedings and does not let the level of excitation get out of control or the commitment and experiential involvement engulf the entire being; in a sense, the ego moves the body.

---

*Rhythm is an inherent quality of life that can be microscopically examined on cellular and tissue levels. The rhythmic capacity of the heart is foundational in its influence on the entire movement of the body.

Mature orgasm is more often experienced as rebirth, renewal, a lifegiving experience, whereas immature orgasm, characterized by structured and compulsive movements, is more apt to be experienced as temporarily pleasureful but still unfulfilling. On the one hand is the fluid, living, spontaneous body allowing feeling to flow and tending to reinforce the unified, integrated, spontaneous experience of body as self, *according to its own principles.* On the other is the impotent, restrictive, nonspontaneous body as ego, denying its own integrity, unique expression, and fulfillment. In the immature, nonspontaneous state the flow of excitation is from the rational to the physical (head to genitals). In the mature, spontaneous state, the flow is from the pelvic area to the entire body. This is an experience in which the organism is moved from within. Spontaneous, ego-less movement, or the kind of movement that was the foundation of our being prior to social conditioning, is the most natural mode of human existence and can serve to reinforce a certain sense of body security because of its integrated and coordinated nature. Engagement in this form of physical activity can result in a refreshed view of human living and moving.

Some persons speak of being moved after an experience of mature orgasm, of experiencing themselves as being one with the universe such as in a visionary experience:

> *Once I had an experience during intercourse which was so different from anything else that I don't think I will ever be satisfied until I experience it again. During this experience, without any effort or trying on my part, my body was moved from within, so to speak and everything was right. There was rhythmic movement and a feeling of ecstasy at being a part of something much greater than myself and finally of reward, of real satisfaction and peace.[2]*

In a similar way, involvement in physical activity grounded in spontaneous movement can provide a person with a particular feeling of oneness with the universe.

> *In the last half mile, something happened which may have occurred only one or two times before or since. Furiously I ran; time lost all semblance of meaning. Distance, time, motion were all one. There was myself, the cement, a vague feeling of legs, and the coming dusk. I tore on. Jack had planned to sound the*

*horn first when a quarter mile remained, and then
again at the completion of the six miles. The first
sound barely reached my consciousness. My running
was a pouring feeling. The final horn sounded. I kept
running. I could have run and run. Perhaps I had
experienced a physiological change, but whatever, it
was magic. I came to the side of the road and gazed,
with a sort of bewilderment, at my friends. I sat on
the side of the road and cried tears of joy and sorrow.
Joy at being alive; sorrow for a vague feeling of
temporalness and a knowledge of the impossibility of
giving this experience to anyone.*[4]

From the two examples cited we can detect the similar
qualities of two kinds of moving experience in which the total
organism is actively involved. In both instances the emphasis is on
pleasure in spontaneous activity. We sense that the body is moving
us. The experiences are intensely personal and sometimes spiritual. Any conscious volitional effort becomes subordinate to an
opening up, a letting go, a giving of oneself to the wisdom of the
body. Both are visionary, grounded in ecstasy, and indicative of the
passionate nature of spontaneous movement.

As described in the previous examples, authentic involvement
in sport and other forms of physical activity can provide an
opportunity to let go and re-engage in such a unifying experience.
To engage in activity that is not fragmented or contradictory
confirms one's own integrity. The process of being moved from
within can result in bodily unity.

In order for this process to come about, a mind-body state that
arbitrarily places ego before body (rational before sensual) must be
reversed. Tension, rigidities, and anxieties concealed by processes
of intellectualization constitute direct denials of the body. By
continuously disregarding the bodily feelings that are authentically
your own, you reinforce and often compound a limited sense of
self-awareness and thereby limit your ability to experience joy and
pleasure. If you continue to deny your body's yearnings for
pleasure and joy (available through involvement in spontaneous,
integrated movement), you deny your own essential nature. By
denying the opportunity for pleasure to occur, you do not allow
yourself to engage in those experiential processes that give life its
true significance and inherent meaningfulness.

Human beings must be in touch with and able to accept the
constant interplay of at least two vital yet contradictory human

energies, one active and irrational, one passive and rational, but both mutually complementary in their continuous interaction. This is the basic human schema of yin and yang—rational and irrational human components. The more one can accept the irrational component of being, the more likely that one will be able to respond naturally and spontaneously to fundamental life situations. If a person is truly in touch with the body and not dependent upon rational faculties, the so-called irrational feelings of the body will make sense. In this way, feelings of irrationality are not threats because they are not experienced as something other than self. A key problem seems to be that the body continuously responds to the callings of an ego-dominated social world. In order to eliminate social roles as the basis of bodily identity, human beings must incorporate a new bodily attitude in which awareness and acceptance of feelings will result in a more joyous self. I am suggesting a new morality, an inner morality whose values are integrity, joy, and passion, based on the principles of self-knowledge and self-acceptance. A cornerstone of this new perspective is the intrinsic motivation of experiencing pleasure and its correlate of irrationally letting go, contrasted with the more common emphasis on rationality, holding back, and more appropriate social behaviors.

The continuous dissociation of body from self in existences that are rigidly controlled by the ego constitutes a split which is nearly schizoid in nature. Those persons who do not, cannot, or will not allow themselves to experience the joy and spontaneity of the authentic self engaged intentionally in meaningful movement deny an inner reality (spontaneous body feelings) from becoming an outer reality (expressed and experienced actualizations). This confusion continues if a split between body and person is arbitrarily supported (not denied). I suggest that this split is fundamental to and indicative of some human relations problems which are grounded in our inability or unwillingness to accept, understand, and trust the spontaneous wisdom of our body and the subsequent outcome of being unable to accept the bodily uniqueness of others as experienced by us.

As is common in many forms of human interacting, we often do not say what we feel. We have a tendency to hold back or soften our responses so as not to hurt the other person. If we were more in touch with and receptive of our feelings, we would find this form of social interaction difficult to continue. On a more personal level, if I am in touch with the feelings of my body, I will not be able to lie to you, I will not be able to contrive, intellectualize, and express something that I do not experience. If I did, it would make me "feel bad." If I attempt to misrepresent myself in this presentation, I would create my own internal conflict in the process of denying my own personal integrity. If I were not in contact with my bodily feelings, I would find it much easier to lie to you; I could lie and experience no internal conflict in the form of physical tension and uneasiness.

The state of natural being implies that you experience yourself as a body-subject and not an ego-center of self-righteous action. I invite you to become *conscious* of that which has been previously *unconscious;* I invite you to expand your *consciousness.* Initially this might require your engaging in a process of self-reflection which will lead you to a fuller insight. As Zen methods suggest, the nature of this new awareness is such that:

> *You see it in a seeing that is not-seeing, a knowing that is not-knowing.*[1]

> *What it is can only be experienced and apprehended but not comprehended and explained in concepts.*[1]

You can get yourself back into this state of being in the world by simply losing your mind and coming to your senses (experiencing the joy and passion of the body). You can be reborn into a new centered state which manifests itself in the unified actualization of the joy and passion found in being one with your body. *Not* with your body as an instrument or object but as a work of art continuously in process—a continuous, on-going, life-giving creation and presentation of your self to the world; a communion of human components with spontaneous joy and passion as the cement.

The pure joy experience can often be found in human movement and sport activities that are not purposeful in a utilitarian sense. In running, for example, we run for the on-going joy of running. We do not necessarily run for health, for a specified time, to cover a certain distance, or whatever else; we just run for the sake of running because we are caught up in the immediacy of this movement. There is no sense of urgency to be over *there;* rather, we shall *be-here-now!* There is no progress involved, just process. If we have any goal whatsoever, it is pleasure in the intentional activity of the moment which is experienced in an on-going fashion such that a purpose, expressed in a temporal sequence as some sort of progress *is not present.* In other words, you are not going anywhere when you run, you are just running. This type of involvement in movement is precisely the kind of acting out of pleasure that I discussed previously.

Conceivably, this expression could be viewed as a psychophysiological extension of our own being if we allow the activity to embrace our whole being, if we totally live the experience. Those who have the openness to grasp this experience will find that its mere presence and your spontaneous involvement imbue it with its own meaningfulness and worthwhileness. All you have to do is let it happen!

REFERENCES

1. Herrigel, E.: *The Method of Zen.* New York: Vintage Books, 1970.
2. Lowen, A.: *Love and Orgasm.* New York: Signet Books, 1965.
3. Lowen, A.: *The Betrayal of the Body.* New York: Collier Books, 1967.
4. Spino, M.: Running as a spiritual experience. In *The Athletic Revolution.* Edited by J. Scott. New York: Macmillan, 1971, pp. 224–225.

Chapter 15

Meditation: An Inner Experience with the Body

Barbara J. Conry

An analysis or investigation that deals with man's inner-world-of-being involves "fringe data" that cannot be described or explained by a mathematical formula or by statistical measurements.[1] Bona fide research that concerns itself with first-person descriptions of how it *feels* and what it *means* to exist as a human being in the world involves vague, changing, and subtle aspects of meaningful experience. Explorations that deal with meaningful experience yield factual data about the subjective, introspective, and intuitive nature of man for which a language for a concept, definition, or category may not yet have been created. These data are evasive and subjective but, nonetheless, genuinely empirical and scientific. Therefore, if we are serious about researching the meaning-structures of meaningful experience, we must keep in mind that man's inner needs and feelings are not necessarily related to what can be gathered in a test tube. There are, for example, both subjective and spiritual forces that penetrate the embodiment of every individual but are omnipotent and incapable of being harnessed and understood by traditional scientific methods.

How is it possible, then, to gain access to these inner forces that comprise the subjective pole of lived experience? Or, how is it that man comes to understand himself as a unique subject, experiencing himself as a pure embodied ego as opposed to an empirical ego? And finally, how is it that man comes to understand the world because of himself rather than to understand himself because of the world? To answer these important ontological questions, I propose a phenomenological approach to meditation. Before describing this philosophical approach toward self-understanding, I will establish groundwork by referring to its "two-prong structure." The following statements represent the essential characteristics of a phenomenological approach to meditation:

1. Meditation requires a particular way of living; the meditator must be willing to engage in a form of introspective analysis—that is, no matter how difficult or painful it may be he must be willing to describe accurately and honestly what "appears" before him in consciousness.
2. Meditation requires that the phenomenological epoch be applied to the act of introspection; by applying the epoch the meditator is able to to describe what "appears" in his field of consciousness without presuppositions and/or emotional biases; thus, the meditator is able to describe the objects of consciousness in their unadulterated form.

YOGA MEDITATION: A PHENOMENOLOGICAL JOURNEY

Through Yoga meditation one gradually learns to control the sense, to disengage oneself from the world, and finally, to turn one's mind inward toward the "pure embodied consciousness" one is, that is, to turn on oneself without falling into the trap of objectifying oneself.* The purpose of meditation is not to make an object or thing of ourselves, but rather to understand ourselves as the subject or the inwardness that we are. How, then, does one achieve access to one's own inwardness? This is accomplished by learning a new and different way of perceiving. For example, our everyday way of thinking, feeling, and perceiving usually extends outward from the embodied ego that "I am" to the outside world—or to anything external that is a reference and appears in the form of otherness. This type of perceiving and thinking that reaches outward might be termed *referential thought.* But when we set out to research and examine our own embodied consciousness, the act of perceiving is no longer directed outward but inward. It involves a way of thinking that goes back into itself; it is a form of self-dialogue that turns on itself. With the use of existential terms, this self-referential researching might be called *reflexive thought;*[1] with an Eastern approach it might be referred to as an *act of meditation.*

An illustration might serve to elucidate these different modes of thinking and perceiving. If we represent awareness as an arrow that always points outward, then referential thought might be symbolized as

* There are various forms of meditation. I offer a phenomenological approach that can be employed for disclosing everyday events and experiences.

$$\text{Embodied ego} \xrightarrow{\text{Act of perceiving}} \text{World,}$$

or to use *Husserl's paradigm**

$$\text{Ego} \xrightarrow{\text{Cogito}} \text{Cogitatum.}$$

Thus, reflective thought expresses that man is directed outwardly; that the subject–world continuum *is being*. If man is to achieve meaning in life, he must be willing to thrust himself outward to experience the world. This is so because man and the world are dialectically related; they are independent but interdependent. Because no object of experience has meaning in and of itself, it is man who illuminates these objects with a particular meaning. As Merleau-Ponty has so profoundly pointed out, the living body secretes within itself a significance and attitude which is then projected outward to all objects of experience.[2] On the other hand, man (as embodied consciousness) is what he is because objects are presented to him; man is always in search of some form of otherness in his world of being. And so referential thought reminds us that consciousness is not restricted to subjectivity (as Cartesianism would have it), but arises through subject–object interaction. Thus, consciousness is the precondition for meaningful being, but meaningful experience itself is the result of a subject–object encounter.

Now let us turn our attention once again to the particular mode of perceiving termed *reflexive thought*. It is this mode of perception that allows the embodied subject to experience a sense of subjectivity; the subject, that is, experiences his own inwardness. However, for reflexive thinking we must look inward rather than outward; not by turning the arrow, but by stepping backward. Although the arrow continues to point to the world, we step backward. By stepping backward, we disengage ourselves from the world, which prevents us from objectifying ourselves with all our worldly surroundings. During a meditative exercise, then, we temporarily remove ourselves from the world in order to come closer to our own subjectivity.

Because man and the world are intimately and fluidly related, it is important that the arrow continue to point outward. The arrow

---

*Edmond Husserl devised the tripartite formula ego-cogito-cogitatum to explain the "intentionality of consciousness."

also serves as a reminder that our disengagement is only temporary. When appropriate (when the meditative exercise has terminated), the subject reconnects with the world. The meditator who finds it necessary to withdraw from the world retains, nevertheless, the capacity to return to the world. His connection with the world (unlike the schizophrenic individual) is never irretrievably broken or out of control. The authentic meditator is always in full command over the structure of this subject–world continuum. Similarly, when the meditator merges into the world (i.e., commits himself to an event, project, idea, goal, or another embodied subject), he retains the capacity to withdraw from it; every individual is susceptible to times that may require a temporary withdrawal from the world. Nonetheless, it is reflexive thinking that is employed during meditation as symbolized in Figure 15–1.

By engaging in the first reduction, an individual steps back onto the arrow and begins to unravel or peel off some of the worldly fringes and personal concomitants attached to his acts of perception. It is the first reduction then, that allows the meditator to first realize his existence as an empirical embodied ego.* Only after initial awareness is the subject able to bracket his role as an empirical embodied ego—only to remove himself from it. Once bracketing has been completed the meditator is ready to engage in a series of reductions in order to experience a pure sense of subjectivity. In other words, by stepping back onto the arrow the subject enables himself to analyze his personal mode of perceiving and reacting to the world. He discloses certain bodily attitudes and feelings that have been injected into various acts of perception. This means that some of the social, emotional, political, attitudinal, and axiological components that circumscribed the meaningful experience, event, or object in question are disclosed. The more successful an individual is at unraveling these personal attachments, as well as distancing himself from the objectivities of the world, the farther he steps back on the arrow, thus coming closer and closer to understanding his pure consciousness. Only after successive reductions is the subject able to retreat from the object (cogitatum) and act (cogito) to rest finally on the ultimate source of apprehension, that is, the pure embodied ego. When the final reduction has been accomplished the meditator will not only experience himself as a pure embodied consciousness, but will also

---

*The term *empirical embodied-ego* refers to the self who has experienced a form of cathexis with the world. Because the embodied-subject has become so attached to the world that he loses contact with his own inwardness, the empirical-self is viewed as a cogitatum or object of experience.

First reduction:

Embodied-ego as
pure consciousness

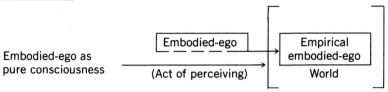

Second reduction:

Pure embodied-ego

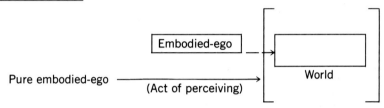

Other reductions:

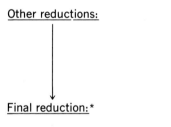

Final reduction:*

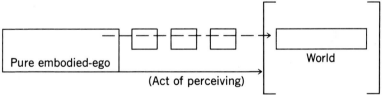

*Only after several successive reductions is one finally able to disclose the pure embodied ego. The number of reductions involved in this form of self-conscious meditation depend on the individual needs of each meditator.

Figure 15–1. Meditative reductions.

come to understand the following pervasive traits about his being-in-the-world:

1. As an embodied subject he plays an active role in all acts of perception; he is the creator and designer of his life-world.

2. As a pure embodied ego he experiences a certain unity and harmony of being—he experiences himself as both mind and body; it is this experience of oneness that encourages the ego to be committed to the body; the pure embodied ego realizes that he sees the world and the world sees him through his body.

3. The way man is concretely living and being his body directly affects the way he is experiencing the world; if he experiences and manipulates his own body like an object (rather than as a subject), then it is likely that he will experience other embodied subjects in a similar fashion. If the body is undernourished because of limited movement experiences, poor nutrition, insufficient sensory stimulation, or a lack of cultural and aesthetic experiences, then one's perceptions of the world might also be experienced in a fixed, dull, and undernourished manner; for example, the embodied subject may find it impossible to change or alter the figure-ground structure of a particular gestalt experience.

4. As a pure consciousness, the embodied subject realizes that "I am my body" rather than "I have a body." This bodily attitude is reflected in the following locutions:

   a. To say that "my body experiences pain" is to say that "I experience pain."

   b. To say that "my body is stuffed and uncomfortable" is to say that "I have chosen to overindulge."

   c. To say that "my nerves are taut" is to say that "I am nervous and anxious about a particular feeling, thought, or event."

To summarize, then, this form of meditation can be practiced by applying the phenomenological epoch to one's everyday way of perceiving, thinking, and feeling. In other words, one must bracket one's strong attachments to the objectivities of the world. In doing so, one is able to trace one's perceptions, feelings, attitudes, and thoughts back to their point of origin. The point of origin is the embodied self (pure consciousness) which is stripped of all its biases, presuppositions, emotional and social attachments, and pragmatic concerns with the everyday world. In this sense meditation involves a phenomenological approach to self-understanding.

It is an effort to describe, without presuppositions and prejudice, what is before us in experience. Furthermore, it can be said that any datum of experience whatever (such as a feeling of depression, guilt or loneliness, the experience of love or opposition, the experience of conflict or cognitive dissonance) can be subjected to a phenomenological examination. Thus, while in a meditative state, a subject might attempt to disclose the truth of certain experiences or events that have already occurred in his life-world. The more successful he is at stepping back from his worldly attachments, the closer he will come to the truth and reality of his experiences. Therefore, the subject must observe the particular experience or event in question from a distance. He must remove himself from his immediate and conscious engagement in it. Only by bracketing, distancing, and reflecting can we see a particular object, event, or experience as it is in itself, that is, as it appears in itself. The epoch is necessary in order to divorce an object from the projections of pragmatic reasoning and the interpretations of our synthesizing consciousness. By bracketing our natural involvement with a particular event, we enable ourselves to analyze something that is closer to us than the event itself (or the object of apprehension), that is, our personal mode of perceiving and reacting to the event. By focusing on the act or mode of perceiving as well as the event (or object) in question, we come closer to understanding our own subjectivity. If we retreat far enough, we come to focus on the embodied subject who is responsible for the *act* itself. In other words, we come to understand the ultimate source of perception or the subjectivity which illuminates all objects of perception. This *phenomenological journey,* then, is what the meditator sets out to accomplish successfully.

REFERENCES

1. Koestenbaum, P.: *The Vitality of Death.* Westport, Conn.: Greenwood Publishing Co., 1971.
2. Merleau-Ponty, M.: *Phenomenology of Perception.* New York: The Humanities Press, 1962.

SELECTED REFERENCES

Behanan, K. T.: *Yoga: A Scientific Evaluation.* New York: Dover Publications, Inc., 1937.
Keyes, K., Jr.: *Handbook to Higher Consciousness.* Berkeley, Calif.: Living Love Center, 1973.
Koestenbaum, P. (Translator): *The Paris Lectures.* The Hague: Martinus Nijhoff, 1970.
Mishra, R. S.: In *The Textbook of Yoga Psychology.* Edited by A. Adman. London: The Lyrebird Press, Ltd. 1972.

SECTION IV

BEING MY SELF

Chapter 16

Introduction

The concept of self as an integral part of personality is probably as old as man himself. Philosophers of early civilizations advanced theories regarding the nature of self, its relationship to behavior, and its importance in social interaction. With the development of the Gestalt-Field theory of movement in the United States, came an emphasis on the study of self as a crucial factor in understanding human behavior.

Self theory is strongly phenomenological in nature and is based on the principle that man reacts to his phenomenal world according to the way he perceives this world. The phenomenal field consists of the totality of experiences of which the person is aware at the instant of behavior. Phenomenal self, which is differentiated from the phenomenal field, includes all those parts of the field that the individual experiences as part or characteristic of self. Self is a doer because it is an aspect of a field that determines behavior, and also an object because it consists of self-experiences. Thus, self is created from the totality of experiences in which perception is primary in both the development and the change of self. The most salient feature of each person's phenomenal world is his self—the self as seen, perceived, and experienced.

Self theory holds that one's behavior is always meaningful, and that we could understand each person's behavior if we could perceive a person's phenomenal world as perceived by that person. Because this is impossible, our closest approximation is to understand the individual's attitudes and concepts of self. Within an existential orientation to self, the self is neither definable nor describable in words; it is known only to the person through experiences of self. One's concept of self is definable only as one experiences self, this definition being an essential factor in growth and actualization of potentials. The attitudes and concept of self are formed from experiential realizations which result from encounters with significant others and with one's environment. Thus, as Allen and Thomas suggest, the investigation of self begins with individual subjective encounters with self rather than with an experimenter's objective, indirect assessment of self.

The first chapter in this section presents the idea that experience is the source of self theory. Dorothy Allen and Carolyn Thomas take the position that experience is the source of meaning, behavior, and self-concept; conversely, meaning, behavior, and self-concept are experienced phenomena. They argue the need for experiential data, if we are to have a fuller understanding of human behavior. In order to have access to experiential data, they suggest the development of a phenomenally objective descriptive method, the identification of behavioral questions that have experiential roots in sport and physical activity, and the acceptance of subjective experience as a valid source of data.

Kleinman advocates a position similar to that of Allen and Thomas when he urges an experiential exploration of self, the "I–me" relationship, to gain better understanding of what is meant when we speak of personal meaning in sport. He pursues the substantiation of sport's potential for productive human effort, and suggests that sport has intrinsic elements which may serve as catalysts for the encouragement of change in one's mode of being, or self-actualization.

In this self-dimension of being in sport, the *person* is considered to be an intervening variable, mediating and influencing responses, a behavioral-human model concerned with the total person. The emphasis is on broader considerations within the sport experience, such as whether one is sufficiently in touch or in contact with one's self to free the potentials that are there; whether one has free access to feelings and emotions and can integrate them with one's intellect; whether one is bound by inner conflicts and stresses or has come to terms with oneself to the point where one can interact freely with external environments; and whether one can share self with others and use such experiences as a means for additional growth and development. The freedom to develop such potential begins with the *self* as the primary reality; it means to begin from premises based on a wholeness of human experience.

Ginny Studer explores the potential for such free access to feelings and emotions in movement experiences. She shares with the reader an experiential subjective description of her experiences of self and the temporal dimension. Studer suggests that her human temporality is explored and extended in movement experiences, and that the exploration and extension of self are an important source for the meaning which she finds in moving. Studer begins with self as the primary reality in her exploration of being human in sport.

Bonnie Beck argues that one cannot be human in sport unless one can focus on one's identity and sexual unity as a whole person; she seeks a removal of all arbitrarily defined sexual inhibitions, and calls on all human beings to be free in their feminine/masculine unity. Beck suggests possibilities for involvement in sport which offer ways to measure ultimate *human* benefits, and suggests further that, if sports are to be a part of the movement toward human liberation, the form and substance of sports must change.

Chapter 17

The Sport Experience and the Experiencing of Self

Dorothy J. Allen
Carolyn E. Thomas

A phenomenon always occurs within a certain context that is relevant to the understanding of the phenomenon in that it is one of the determiners of the meaning of the phenomenon. Laing has suggested that there is a split between experience and behavior; the inner is split from the outer. Because without inner experience outer behavior loses its meaning and without outer behavior, inner experience loses its substance. The research of self-concept in physical activity has assumed a split between experience and behavior and has not explored the human being in movement in the total sense; meaning, feeling, and experiencing have not been sources of data.

The framework shown in Figure 17–1 delimits the position of a humanistic view of self-concept and sports and its examination in this chapter.

The assumptions underlying the humanistic view of self-concept and sport and its examinations are:

1. Meaning and feeling are intimately related to behavior.
2. Meaning and behavior in the experiential mode have gestalt characteristics.

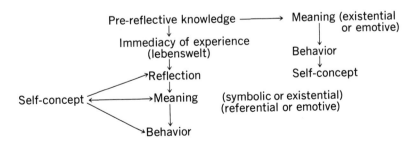

Figure 17–1.

135

3. The reality of experience and the personal creations of the individual can never be fully known in analysis and abstraction nor by precise measurement, but only through a meaningful integration and reflection on immediate experience.

4. Maintenance and enhancement of the self-concept are the fundamental human motives: behavior can be understood in terms of these activities.

5. Self-concept functions as an operational base for behavior, an evaluative structure, a source of experience, and an experienced phenomenon. One's interactions with the world cannot be separated from interactions with one's vital being.

6. Experience is the source of meaning, behavior, and self-concept; conversely, meaning, behavior, and self-concept are experienced phenomena.

7. In order for change to occur, there must be a change in experiencing or in the perception of the experience.

8. Behaviors in movement experiences are highly personalized and involve experiences of self-identification.

The gap between having many data *about* a person and a real understanding *of* that person has long been a source of controversy among psychologists and others who ask questions about human behavior. Data *about* a person assume a study of man as an objective being with quantitative characteristics. The identification of such quantities has led to a further assumption that such data will explain behavior. Man studied only in an objective way is no longer a human person. In the behavioral sciences, man plays a double role: object to be explored and exploring person. In modern science, man, the observer, has been reintroduced onto the scene of observation. Because science, with its measurement of time and other conditions, is *founded in human nature*, it seems improbable that human nature could be fully explored with the methods of science. Man as a scientist cannot, with his peculiar methods and techniques, draw a self-portrait of the scientist as a man. *Verification requires the verifier to act in the lebenswelt.* Thus, if one is interested in studying characteristics of *human* phenomena, the qualitative dimensions must be considered. Qualitative questions are asked of man as an experiencing being.

The hangover of logical positivism into this decade is causing us to seek abstract and absolute answers to highly complex experiences, with the result that meaning-laden encounters are distilled to a condition of artificial purity. The concern of the humanist dealing with sport and movement experiences does not lend itself to analysis, for the ground is as important as the figure because figure arises out of ground. In other words, the phenomenon cannot be studied outside the context in which it appears and still be the same phenomenon. Experiential data must be collected to ascertain what figure is to ground and to have a fuller understanding *of* human behavior; the experiential-behavioral relationship of the subject must be studied.

In a discussion of the appropriateness or inappropriateness of the scientific method, it should be pointed out that it is a fallacy to assume that all sciences and all scientific methods are alike. Indeed, as Oppenheimer suggests, the language and tools of one science are not applicable to another.[16] Physics and chemistry with different purposes and problems use a different set of "tools." It is even further folly and a compounding of absurdities to study man with inappropriate methods. "An approach which says facts are facts, such as behaviorism, is impractical and meaningless. If we are to study man as he is, then we must formulate a new kind of knowledge, one which is primarily personal rather than technical."[18] Kleinman, after Heisenberg, warns that new laws and perhaps even new language are necessary in the study of a new phenomenon (sport) in which man is a subject and the transferral of old laws to new endeavors is simply not appropriate.

> *In an attempt to examine movement, our researchers have adopted the "tried and true" methods of physiology. But understanding movement skill ability and its acquisition is incomplete to say the least and incorrect to say the most without regard for the living subject. This, of necessity, calls for a psychology of movement; one which is not based on the principles of physiology and physics but, in dealings with the lived movement, must accept the challenge of developing principles of its own.*[11]

Kleinman's call for method in understanding skill applies to all aspects of movement, behavior, and maybe even more important, to concerns of meaning, behavior, and self-concept. The call for an examination of the experiential base of and by the living subject closely parallels the position and dimensions Maslow identified for existential psychology.

*It lays great stress on starting from experiential
knowledge rather than from systems of concepts or
abstract categories or a prioris. It lays as a foundation
personal subjective experience upon which abstract
knowledge may be built and upon which reflection
may occur.*[14]

Privette, from a study exploring factors associated with human
functioning which transcends modal behavior, found that clear
focus on the self and the object, and the relationship between the
two was an important factor for transcendent functioning.[19] Self,
object, and relationship are all perceived in integrated, meaningful,
sharp focus. The person holds figure in bold contrast to ground,
thereby apprehending the focused object fully, both perceptually
and cognitively. The psychological experience is described as one
that subsumes a clear identity of self. In experiencing clearly and
strongly something other than oneself, one experiences self with
great clarity, thus the importance of the functional relationship to
the definition of self. A more detailed examination of the
methodological possibilities will be delineated later in this
chapter.

Both theoretically and behaviorally, self-concept is a highly
complex aspect of personality. It has both cognitive (self-awareness
or self-knowledge) and affective (esteem, self-regard, self-cathexis)
components. It has at least four orientations: the actual self
(objective assessment), the perceived self (myself as I really am),
the ideal self (myself as I would like to be), and the self as
perceived to be perceived by others (myself as I think others see
me). Thus, when both components and the four orientations are
considered, there is a minimum of eight ways of experiencing self
that are part of the total self-concept. In addition to these variables,
there seem to be at least two other separate but interrelated aspects
of the self, namely, body and movement, which may change with
the specific situation.[1] Most research has been directed toward a
quantitative assessment of self-concept with little recognition of
the qualitative-experiential sources of concept. For the purposes of
most research, the self-concept refers to how the individual
perceives himself in all facets of life.

According to some self theorists, the self is defined as the
person's attitudes and feelings toward himself. The self, then, is
what the person thinks of himself. According to Jersild, the self
includes the individual's ideas of what he looks like and his ideas of
how he affects others.[8] The self includes the meaning of one's

distinctive characteristics, abilities, and resources. The self also includes attitudes, feelings, and values one holds about oneself, one's self-esteem and self-reproach, or both. From this definition emerges the idea of self-concept that forms the core around which all facets of personality are organized. Consequently, what a person thinks of himself is the prime determiner of his behavior. The self is an aspect of all one's experience while contributing to the quality and form of all one's experiences.

Combs and Snygg's phenomenal self is not only an objective being but also an experiencing being.[3] All behavior is completely determined by and pertinent to the "phenomenal field" of the individual. The phenomenal field consists of the totality of experiences of which the person is aware at the instant of behavior. The phenomenal self, which is differentiated from the phenomenal field, includes all parts of the field that the individual experiences as part or characteristic of himself. The self is an experiencing being because it is an aspect of the field that determines behavior and is experiencing such behavior, yet it is also an object because it consists of self experiences. Thus, self-concept is created from the totality of experiences in which perception is primary in both the development and change of self-concept. All experiences of the individual are organized into some relationship to self, ignored because they have no perceived relationship to self, or given distorted symbolization because they are inconsistent with the self structure. The end point of personality development is a basic congruence between the phenomenal field of experience and the conceptual structure of self.

According to Schutz, cognitive reality of self is embodied in the processes of subjective human experiences.[20] All direct experiences of human beings are in and of the life-world, in the whole sphere of everyday experiences, orientations, and actions.

> ... *man does not simply find himself in a specific situation; this situation is an episode in his on-going life. He stands in it as a person having gone through the long chain of his prior life experiences. . . . subjectively, no two persons could possibly experience the same situation in the same way . . . each has entered this present situation with his own purposes and the concomitant appraisals are rooted in his past. . . .*[20]

Situation refers to a phenomenological environment rather than a purely physical environment. Situations are psychologically defined by self as they take on meaning. Situations do not exist abstractly but in relation to a person.

As Moustakas notes, in a more existential sense, one's self-concept is definable only as one experiences one's self; this definition is an essential factor in one's growth and actualization of potentials.[15] Self-concept is formed from experiential realizations resulting from encounters with significant others and with one's environment.[6] Thus, the investigation of self begins with the individual's subjective encounters with self rather than with an experimenter's objective, indirect assessment of self, as is the case with projective techniques and self report. According to Jourard, "To be a self is to be, not an object, but the subject of one's own experiencing."[9]

Gendlin has stated that individuals who change in a fundamental way are characterized by a change in their inner feelings and their experiencing of felt meanings.[7] A study by Fuerst, which dealt with fundamental change in persons, explored a kind of experience that may contribute to positive health.[6] Fuerst identified the experience as a "turning point experience," and found that the importance of a positive turning point experience is perceived by an individual in its effect on self in contrast to its effect on relationships to environment or to other persons. He speculated from the results that self-concept was a factor that influenced the nature of the turning point experience, that is, the experience being negative for one person and positive for another. Fitts has noted that there is a relationship between a person's self-concept and the way that he reacts to life's happenings.[5] People with positive self-concepts have been found to be able to use both negative and positive experiences to enhance their psychological growth. Vargas, in his study of positive experiencing and behaving, suggests the same conclusion.[22] He further implys that self-concept is most strikingly affected by (1) experiences, especially interpersonal experiences that generate positive feelings and a sense of value and worth; (2) competence in areas that are valued by the individual and others; and (3) self-actualization, or the realization of one's potentialities. Self-concept, then, is understood in terms of the experience from which it emerges.

Krueger has stated:

> *Everything distinguishable in experience is interconnected, embedded within a total-whole that penetrates and envelops it. The experience-qualities of this total-whole are the feelings and emotions.*[12]

> *Phenomenologically, all complex-qualities have some-thing in common: they spread over all conscious awareness; they deny indifference . . . one set of events, the objects of my feelings, is always related to the other set, my feelings themselves. Feelings are the complex-qualities of the experienced totality.*[12]

> *Every dissection of the total experience destroys the whole and is fundamentally in discord with it.*[12]

Potentially experience can become the source for self theory. There is a need for both new questions of behavior in physical activity (questions of feeling, meaning, and experiencing relative to self-concept) and the methods that will allow a fruitful examination of such behavioral questions. Phenomenological study that ex-plores the experience of motivation (being "turned on") in sport and the experience of self in such experiences may be a valid inquiry. What are the consequences of these moments of intense experiencing? Other inquiry may be directed toward the ex-periential-behavioral dimensions of self-structure, which may parallel the processes of learning sport or other motor skills, or toward the core (central) or peripheral attitudes of women and men who have deep feelings of personal inadequacy in physical activity. Whom are the individuals who find physical activity and bodily expression so inconsistent with their self-structures? Performance scores reveal little about the performer as a person or how meaningful the performance or the score was to the self-structure of the individual. Perhaps the initiation of some studies exploring the individual's experiences in sport rather than his performance scores would be enlightening relative to self-concept study.

If it is assumed that a meaningful experience occurs in sport, and that it evokes an affective response in expression and behavior, can this response be satisfactorily explained or described? Pless-ner, in stating that "it is only behavior which explains the body,"[17] and Moustakas, who states that "experience is real only when it is lived; as soon as it is talked about or defined, the living moment is lost,"[5] would seem to suggest that the lebenswelt cannot be suffi-ciently explained. Straus argues that the primary barrier in attempt-ing to express the nature of the immediate experience is lan-guage. It is "sheer self-deception to believe that reports of experi-mental subjects are able to transmit to us the subjects' immediate experiences intact."[21] Similarly, involvement in sport or any other intense experience suggests the impossibility of full explanation of the experience. Participation in the activity of sport itself, as it involves the player, transcends intellectualization by escaping obtuse abstractions. Sport is one experience that demands total involvement of mind, body, and emotions to achieve success, and is perhaps unique as a phenomenon making these demands. The study of self-concept and behavior in this context may provide a wealth of data applicable to other aspects of learning and behavior.

Before completely discounting the possibility of describing the sport experience or sport lebenswelt or negating the value of even attempting to do so, it seems necessary to examine the nature of description and what it entails with regard to the one who describes and the one who must evaluate the description, as well as the potential data to be examined. The nature of a description of the lebenswelt can be said to be the appreciation, recognition, and reflective awareness of the qualities in the object or medium, rather than the object or medium per se. This suggests that the description is not analytically reductive nor quantitatively measurable. It does suggest cognition of an affective or a qualitative experience. Qualitative reflective awareness can result from an affective response and a recognition of the *significance* that the response has for the individual.

With Walsh's model, which is a definition of the essence of the aesthetic experience and aesthetic description, the following discussion is an exploration of the nature and value of the reflective description of the sport lebenswelt.[23] Walsh starts her discussion from the unstated but implied premise that the aesthetic description is a verbal or linguistic description. Although Straus cited the ineptitude of language in describing the "lived experience," it must be considered that language has never been effective in describing any affective response, thus creating what Plessner has called the "marginal expressions" of laughing and crying and the many modes which fall in between. Language may also be considered inept in even the logical, rational, and cognitive contexts and potentialities. Linguistic inefficiency should not preclude attempts to describe as closely as possible the experiential mode, although it must be granted that words have their limitations. Despite the indefinability of sport and the limitations of logical and linguistic description it may be possible to state that

> engagement in game, sport, or art, and a description
> of this kind of engagement enable us to know what
> game, sport, or art is on a level that adds another
> dimension to our knowing. . . . Experiential descrip-

tion renders significance to a concept different in kind
from linguistic utility.[10]

Description borders on being affective and must be considered to
be connotative rather than denotative.[23]

A necessary but not sufficient condition for the description to
be valid is that it be phenomenally objective. "Aesthetic descriptions, whatever else they may be, are of the 'it is' rather than the 'I
am' character."[23] Phenomenal subjectivity is the quality or characteristic "in you," whereas phenomenal objectivity is the quality
perceived in the object or in the experience. Although, as Bergson
suggested, the sadness of the song may be "in you," what is
described is not "you" or the "thing" but what happened between
you and the thing. The description is of the experience and not of
one or another of the components. Examination of the description
of this bond by the observer may lead to an understanding of how
the subject views himself in the experience. Phenomenal subjectivity can be likened to Dewey's charge that, although emotion is
present in the aesthetic experience, its expression is objective,
whereas a mere emotional discharge is subjective. Pure subjectivity in describing an affective state is equivalent to sentiment and
cannot be considered a valid description for ascertaining meaning
or behavior. However, it does seem possible that the description
can and should be guided by the investigator to elicit a
phenomenally objective description.

"The aesthetic attitude involves a certain detachment, a
detachment sufficient to preclude purely personal association."[23]
Although Walsh was viewing this detachment in the audience
sense, a certain detachment is possible for the athlete. Reflection
after the experience provides a degree of detachment in that the
performer becomes audience to his own act. Although the personal
association is never removed, it is possible to take an objective
view of the experience and remove it from the realm of sentiment.
It is true that reflection on one's performance remains subjective
unless specific criteria by which the performance may be judged
are fulfilled. And it is also true that subjective and reflective
reporting are subject to inaccuracy depending on the honesty of the
participant. However, in the experiential realm of meaning and the
behavior that may result, any attempt to describe or measure the
experience from outside is subject to even more erroneous
reporting.

Experiential phenomenological description resists definition
in casual terms. Although it is a "bracketing out" of affective

essences, it is not a reduction of these essences nor of the experience to any series of facts, laws, or universal truths. Descriptive expressions of "feeling and emotion are affirmations of our attitudes toward situations. The pure description of a feeling is the definition of a human being in his well-defined attitude toward the situation."[2] To have experienced the situation is to have an insight into the situation and the feelings created by the situation. As Bannister pointed out, it is almost impossible to describe a rose to someone who has never seen a rose. One can read Herzog's *Annapurna* and *think* that he must have felt joy at reaching the top of Annapurna and, like good description or narrative, it can move the listener or reader. However, if the reader has climbed any mountain, even though it was not Annapurna, there is an insight into the feelings, the situation, and the description that the words cannot render but that "having been there" in whatever limited sense can convey to the observer.

Perhaps the development of a phenomenally objective descriptive method, the identification of behavioral questions with experiential roots in sport and physical activity, and the acceptance of subjective experience as a valid source of data may provide students of behavior with a new tool for a broader and more accurate view of self-concept and its relationship to meaning and behavior.

REFERENCES

1. Allen, D., and Burton, E.: Comparative Study of Selected Student Population on State and Trait Anxiety, Self, Body, and Movement Cathexis. Unpublished study, 1971.
2. Buytendijk, F. J. J.: The phenomenological approach to feeling and emotion. In *Psychoanalysis and Existential Philosophy*. Edited by H. M. Ruitenbeek. New York: E. P. Dutton, 1962.
3. Combs, A., and Snygg, D.: *Individual Behavior*. New York: Harper & Row, 1949.
4. Ecker, D.: Research in Creative Activity, N.A.P.E.C.W. Workshop Report. Washington, D.C.: National Association of Physical Education for College Women, 1964.
5. Fitts, W. H., et al.: The Self-Concept and Self-Actualization. Monograph Series: Studies on the Self-Concept and Rehabilitation, Research Grant SRS No. RD–2419–G. Nashville: Dede Wallance Center, 1971.
6. Fuerst, R. E.: Turning Point Experiences. Unpublished doctoral dissertation. Gainesville, Fla.: University of Florida, 1965.
7. Gendlin, E.: *Experiencing and the Creation of Meaning*. New York: Free Press of Glencoe, 1962.
8. Jersild, A.: *Child Psychology*, 5th ed. Englewood Cliffs, N.J.: Prentice-Hall, Inc., 1960.
9. Jourard, S. (Ed.): *To Be or Not To Be: Existential-Psychological Perspectives on the Self*. Gainesville, Fla.: University of Florida Press, 1967. Social Sciences Monograph No. 34.

10. Kleinman, S.: Toward a non-theory of sport. *Quest, X*:31, 1968.
11. Kleinman, S.: Physical Education and Lived Movement. Unpublished paper presented to National College Physical Education Association for Men. Portland, Ore.: 1970.
12. Krueger, F.: The essence of feeling. In *The Nature of Emotion*. Edited by M. B. Arnold. Baltimore: Penguin Books, 1968.
13. Laing, R. D.: *The Politics of Experience*. New York: Ballentine Books, 1967.
14. Maslow, A.: *Toward a Psychology of Being*. Princeton, N.J.: Van Nostrand Insight Books, 1962.
15. Moustakas, C.: *Creativity and Conformity*. New York: Van Nostrand, 1966.
16. Oppenheimer, R.: *Science and the Common Understanding*. London: Oxford University Press, 1954.
17. Plessner, H.: *Laughing and Crying*. Translated by J. S. Churchill. Evanston, Ill.: Northwestern University Press, 1970.
18. Polanyi, M.: *The Study of Man*. London: Routledge and Kegan, 1959.
19. Privette, G.: Factors Associated with Functioning Which Transcends Model Behavior. Unpublished doctoral dissertation. Gainesville, Fla.: University of Florida, 1964.
20. Schutz, A.: *On Phenomenology and Social Relations*. Edited by H. Wagner. Chicago: University of Chicago Press, 1970.
21. Straus, E.: *Phenomenological Psychology*. New York, Basic Books, 1966.
22. Vargas, R.: A Study of Certain Personality Characteristics of Male College Students Who Report Frequent Positive Experiencing and Behaving. Unpublished doctoral dissertation. Gainesville, Fla.: University of Florida, 1968.
23. Walsh, D.: Aesthetic descriptions. *Br. J. Aesthetics, 10*:237, 1970.

SELECTED READING

Burton, E., and Allen, D.: An Analysis of the Relationship Between State and Trait, Anxiety and Self, Body and Movement Cathexis. Unpublished study, 1971.
Nelson, B., and Allen, D.: A scale for the appraisal of movement satisfaction. *Perceptual Motor Skills, 31*:795, 1970.
Secord, P., and Jourard, S.: The appraisal of body cathexis: Body cathexis and self. *J. Consulting Psychology, 17*:343, 1953.

Chapter 18

Kinesis and the Concept of Self in Sport

Seymour Kleinman

> *Man is spirit. But what is spirit? Spirit is the self.*
> *But what is the self? The self is a relation which*
> *relates itself to its own self, or it is that in the relation*
> *(which accounts for it) that the relation relates itself*
> *to its own self; the self is not the relation but (consists*
> *in the fact) that the relation relates itself to its own*
> *self. Man is a synthesis of the infinite and the finite, of*
> *the temporal and the eternal, of freedom and neces-*
> *sity, in short, it is a synthesis. A synthesis is a relation*
> *between two factors. So regarded, man is not yet a*
> *self.*
>
> *Søren Kierkegaard:* Sickness Unto Death

I continue to be amazed and intrigued by the unintentional appropriateness of the writings of a number of philosophers to the nature of sport. In the course of developing my thoughts for this chapter, I came across a volume dealing with Søren Kierkegaard's conception of the self.[2] Pursuing this further, I went directly to the source, and in his work *Philosophical Fragments*[3] Kierkegaard uses some rather remarkably appropriate terms considering the fact that things such as sport and physical education, in all likelihood, never entered his mind.

For example, Kierkegaard uses the word *kinesis* to categorize a fundamental change in the mode of being, or what may be termed an *existential change*. Kinesis, of course, is the Greek word for motion. For the physical education theorist (at least this one), this is more than enough motivation to stimulate thought. I intend to explore this point more fully later in this chapter. However, it is sufficient to say at this time, without getting too far ahead of myself, that equating the word *kinesis* to a fundamental change in being offers a promising direction for investigation and analysis.

THE I-ME RELATIONSHIP

I should like to point out at the outset that my major emphasis here is on *self,* that is, the personal self manifested in both a public and a private way. It occurs to me that one may call this approach an exploration of the "I-me" relationship. This is probably true, but I do not mean for it to be taken in an egotistical sense, but rather as a focus of serious examination of *self.* Obviously, self cannot be divorced from environment or from things and other selves in the environment. However, without losing sight of this, it is the personal self with which I wish to deal. I think this tack shows some promise for gaining better understanding of what we mean when we speak of personal meaning in sport.

I wish to use the categories Kierkegaard developed in his explication of the concept of self. In no way am I implying that my use and development of these categories reflect or adhere to Kierkegaard's views. To determine these, I would encourage you to go to the source. I am using the categories for my own ends because I believe they may help illustrate and substantiate my own conviction of sport's enormous potential for productive human effort. And this potential deserves serious consideration as a valid means for self-actualization and fulfillment.

I shall begin this investigation of self by developing the distinction between what may be called the traditional concept of self and the self as Kierkegaard describes it. After this discussion, I shall use the categories of infinite and finite, freedom and necessity, and temporal and eternal, which Kierkegaard developed as he set forth his definition of man. It would be helpful to keep in mind throughout this chapter my contention that man in the state of becoming a self is in *motion* from *nonbeing* to *being,* in motion from *possibility* to *actuality,* in motion from *essence* to *existence.* Man is born with the potential to become a self. But it is only through motion of this nature that the self may be realized. It is through *kinesis* that self may become a self.

In addition, I shall try to illuminate the discussion throughout by offering appropriate examples of the sport experience. Indeed, I feel it necessary to state at this point, much to the chagrin of my empirical-minded colleagues, that I regard these experiential descriptions not only as examples but as valid evidence on which claims may be made and conclusions drawn.

THE SELF

The problem of self "emerges at times of 'cosmic homelessness,' times when the structures of meaning . . . begin to crumble.

When the metaphysical home in which man dwells secure begins to collapse, the problem of self appears with all its existential urgency."[2] It was this urgency which, I am certain, motivated Kierkegaard, and it is the kind of urgency that I believe is present today. It is revealed in contemporary religious movements, philosophy, literature, music (all of the arts for that matter), and in a very real sense, I see it emerging in sport. The evidence of our concern for self in sport is becoming more and more abundant. I should like to quote a passage from a little article which appeared recently in a local American Youth Hostel Chapter newsletter.

> *When I first started boating, I thought my satisfaction and elation came from competing with the river and winning. I would attack it again and again, trying evermore difficult maneuvers. True, sometimes I would lose a battle and occasionally I or my boat would be wounded. But such bruises were worth it when my victories came and the feelings of exhilaration filled my body. Occasionally, I would even have delusions of winning the war over this inanimate river. Finally, however, I came to the realization that it is not a struggle between me and the river. The river, with all its dynamic action, is only a catalyst. Boating is a means of self-expression and my competition with the river is me overcoming myself, affirming myself, and realizing myself in my struggle toward victory, toward the absolute, toward self-control.*
>
> *One feels here an intimacy with a powerful surrounding nature which is intensely invigorating in the soul, yet simultaneously calming; in some ways, a deeply religious feeling not easily or often found.*[5]

I intend to return to this passage later, but for the moment let it serve as an introduction to the examination of the concept of the self and some of Kierkegaard's views on the matter.

In the usual holistic terms of the modern (and not so modern) physical education theorist, man is described as a unity of body and soul, or what has been termed a *psychosomatic unity*, with body signifying "the physical aspect of human being, and soul, the affective or psychological aspect."[2] For Kierkegaard this is a "negative unity," a passive sort of existence. The classic concept of body–soul unity is an *immediate* relationship of self. It is the self of the *"immediate* man . . . and it has only an *illusory* (italic mine) appearance of possessing in it something eternal. Thus, the self coheres immediately with 'the other,' wishing, desiring, enjoying, etc., but passively. . . . Its dialectic is: the agreeable and the disagreeable; its concepts are: good fortune, misfortune, fate."[4]

Elaboration and development of this definition are in order, because I think they will affirm what I believe to be the ability of the sport experience to provide this kinetic change of which we are speaking, or a change in one's mode of being.

THE INFINITE AND THE FINITE

Kierkegaard regards a synthesis to be a *relation* between two factors. For self to become a self a dialectical relationship must be established between the finite and infinite. Kierkegaard cautions against the danger of self falling into despair owing to the lack of both finitude and infinitude.

"While one sort of despair plunges wildly into the infinite and loses itself, a second sort permits itself to be defrauded by 'the others.' "[4] The first form leads the self into a "fantastic existence in abstract endeavor after infinity."[4] This plunge into the infinite is the height of essence but is the negation of existence. It is the perpetual "high" into the realm of fantasy. It is not a self realized but a self in essence only.

The second form of self that pursues the *finite* leads to the despair of a man forgetting himself, "forgetting what his name is (in the divine understanding of it), not daring to believe in himself, finding it too venturesome a thing to be himself, far easier and safer to be like the others, to become an imitation, a number, a cipher in the crowd."[4]

However, the world of sport seems to present opportunities in abundance for the realization of self. The dialectic of essence and existence, mediate and immediate, finite and infinite is always present. In effect, it remains only for the participant to seize the opportunity. And it appears that many do so. The sport experience is a continuous ongoing dialectical relationship with the world as present and the world as potential. Sport maintains the perpetual challenge between what is and what might be. It serves as the catalyst that can maintain and encourage synthesis of the self of mediacy and immediacy, the self of finitude and infinitude, the self of concrete and abstract.

"The central dialectic of selfhood is the relation between the body–soul entity and Spirit."[2] It is this relationship between man and God that enables man to gain glimpses of the infinite from his finite stance in the world. It surfaces at extraordinary moments in sport, causing participants to speak of a "deeply religious feeling not easily or often found."

But this is not the self giving rise to *kinesis* (the fundamental change in being). Were the self to be constituted only of this unity of soul and body, it would be merely a thing that is acted on. It would be a self ruled and determined by extrinsic forces alone. Selfhood, however, is more than elements of the natural world subject only to being randomly buffeted about. Kierkegaard introduces a third force, a power not identical to either body or soul, but one that establishes a relationship between this passive and immediate self to what he terms man's "own self." This is what he means when he states that this relationship "relates itself to its own self (and) the relationship is then the positive third term, and this is the self."[2]

In becoming his own self a person thus realizes the potential to be, which Kierkegaard insists is present in us all. This becoming, this relationship, necessitates a fundamental change in mode of being. This power or spirit is not just an additional element introduced into a person's makeup. It is the radical existential and dialectical process which has been referred to previously as kinesis.

At this point and in the light of what I have just described, I should like to develop a personal hypothesis about what all of this may signify for gaining insight into the sport experience, a problem of no little magnitude. Kinesis, as we have been using the term here, most assuredly cannot be used synonymously with physical motion, that is, motion of the body or any of its parts. Nor may it be claimed that this state of kinesis is achieved by combining psychological drives, motives, and operants with resultant behavior manifestations. Kinesis, or what I prefer to call *authentic kinetic change*, is revealed in extraordinary moments of one's life; moments when a relationship "relates itself to its own self." I suggest that ample evidence of this exists in surprisingly large amounts in the world of sport. In fact, one might even contend that sport has intrinsic elements within it which may serve as a catalyst for encouraging this change in being or self-actualization.

Man engages in sport and athletics in neither a casual nor an accidental manner. There is purpose and meaning in "this intensity, this absorption, this power of maddening," as Huizinga has described it. And I believe it is revealed when sport is viewed as providing a means for moments when a relationship "relates itself to its own self." I do not believe it accidental that phrases such as "my competition is me overcoming myself, affirming myself, realizing myself" appear in one manner or another in experiential descriptions of sport. The phrase "deeply religious feeling not easily or often found" should be considered as an appropriate piece of evidence for Kierkegaard's contention that man is a "synthesis of the infinite and the finite, of the temporal and the eternal, of freedom and necessity."[4]

FREEDOM AND NECESSITY

> *You call the signals. You say the strategy. You execute the maneuvers. You make on-the-spot improvisations and adjustment to suit the situation of the moment. Add to these things the fact that no two waves are the same. . . . A solitary person, an individual, meeting unique challenge after unique challenge.*[1]

Kierkegaard contends, as we have seen, that man is a synthesis of freedom and necessity. Now the question is, "does the self become a self (does kinesis occur) by necessity or with freedom?" His answer is that the act of coming into being is not a necessary one but a possible one. Becoming a self, the kinetic change, is movement from possibility to actuality. "The transition takes place with freedom. Becoming is never necessary."[3]

The kinetic change is an existential one, not one of essence. It is free not determined. Nowhere is this freedom more clearly manifested than in sport. "*You* call the signals. *You* lay the strategy. *You* make the improvisations and adjustments." The description captures clearly the freedom inherent in self becoming a self.

However, as in the case of the infinite and the finite, both poles of the dialectic must be present to maintain the synthesis. Self can be lost in the despair of possibility or of necessity.

> *If possibility outruns necessity . . . the self becomes an abstract possibility which tries itself out with foundering . . . but does not budge from the spot. . . . To become is a movement from the spot, but to become oneself is a movement at the spot.*[4]

In the abstract despair of possibility all becomes more and more intense so that nothing ever becomes actualized.

> *At the instant something appears possible, and then a new possibility makes its appearance, at last this phantasmagoria moves so rapidly that it is as if everything were possible—and this is precisely the last moment, when the individual becomes for himself a mirage.*[4]

On the other hand, the lack of possibility or freedom results in the self falling into the despair of necessity.

> *The determinist or the fatalist is in despair, and in despair he has lost his self, because for him everything is necessary. . . . Personality is a synthesis of possibility and necessity. The condition of its survival is therefore analogous to breathing (respiration) which is an in- and an a-spiration. The self of the determinist cannot breathe, for it is impossible to breathe necessity alone, which taken pure and simple suffocates the human self.*[4]

The ultimate act, for Kierkegaard, is self-realization and, in the synthesis of freedom and necessity, is the belief that for God all things are possible.

> *Whether he who is engaged in this fight will be defeated, depends solely and alone on whether he has the will to procure for himself possibility, that is to say, whether he will believe.*[4]

Indeed, it would be presumptuous here to imply that sport lends itself in greater measure to enhance achievement of a man–God relationship than any other form of activity. However, it is undeniable that sport can be an intensely personal and spiritual experience, and it does demonstrate the inventiveness of human imagination to "procure possibility."

> *I tore on. . . . My running was a pouring feeling. I could have run and run. . . . It was magic. I came to the side of the road and gazed, with a sort of bewilderment, at my friends. I sat on the side of the road and cried tears of joy and sorrow. Joy at being alive; sorrow for a vague feeling of temporalness, and a knowledge of the impossibility of giving this*

> *experience to anyone. . . . I have never understood*
> *what occurred that late afternoon: whether it was*
> *just a fine run . . . or finding out who and what I was*
> *through a perfect expression of my own art form. It*
> *still remains a mystery.*[6]

THE TEMPORAL AND THE ETERNAL

It is when dealing with self as an eternal element of human existence that Kierkegaard issues his most formidable challenge. The task he sets is for self to become conscious of itself as spirit. This is, of course, what he regards as eternal.

> *Every human existence which is not conscious of*
> *itself as spirit—in obscurity about itself, takes its*
> *faculties merely as active powers, without in a deeper*
> *sense being conscious whence it has them, which*
> *regards itself as an inexplicable something which is to*
> *be understood from without—every such existence,*
> *whatever it accomplishes, though it be the most*
> *amazing exploit, whatever it explains, though it were*
> *the whole of existence, however, it enjoys life*
> *aesthetically—every such existence is after all de-*
> *spair.*[4]

Heroic deeds and exploits are only examples of the soul–body synthesis in every man. Without consciousness of the eternal, a man is merely *immediate*. He exists on the temporal plane only.

It is, of course, difficult to say whether sport provides a means of access for the self to recognize itself as spirit. This is so personal and private an aspect of human experience that only through the intimacy of self-examination and self-knowledge may one be certain. However, it is interesting to note that in the preceding description the runner expresses sorrow for the "vague feeling of temporalness" which returns after the experience, the implication being that there was an eternal element in the act he had just completed. Therefore, it does not seem accidental at all that he entitled his description "Running As a Spiritual Experience."

For Kierkegaard, man is spirit and spirit is the self. But man is also a synthesis which is only a relationship between two factors. Thus, a synthesis alone is not enough for self to become a self. Becoming a self involves a "coming into existence" kind of change (kinesis) which "is not a change in essence but in being and is a transition from not existing to existing."[3]

What I have attempted to demonstrate in this chapter is that the kinds of movement activity manifested in the sport experience may be closely allied to authentic kinetic change; indeed it may serve to enhance it. Although I feel obliged to urge caution against overgeneralizing, I encourage you, also, to let the experiences speak for themselves.

REFERENCES

1. Allen, J.: *Locked In: Surfing for Life.* New York: Barnes & Noble, 1970.
2. Cole, P. J.: *The Problematic Self in Kierkegaard and Freud.* New Haven: Yale University Press, 1971.
3. Kierkegaard, S.: *Philosophical Fragments*, 2nd ed. Princeton, N.J.: Princeton University Press, 1967.
4. Kierkegaard, S.: *The Sickness unto Death.* Garden City, N.Y.: Doubleday & Co., Anchor Books, 1954.
5. Marine, M.: Why We Boat Rivers. *The Buckeye Hostler,* Columbus Council, American Youth Hostels, June 1972.
6. Spino, M.: Running as a spiritual experience. In *The Athletic Revolution.* Edited by J. Scott. New York: The Free Press, 1971.

Chapter 19

Moment-to-Moment Experiences of Self

Ginny Studer

Time permeates all human experience, fashioning the process of life and defining the inevitability of death. I am a temporal being, not by reason of some vagary of the human makeup, but by virtue of an inner necessity. All endurance or transience seems relative to human temporality, and perhaps above all, to my individual life span. All things other than possibly the primary infinitesimals are always changing, but because the change is fast or slow, obvious or hidden, drastic or minor, I identify some as enduring and others as being transient. I speak of the everlasting hills, but, of course, they sink and rise. I speak of the eternal stars, but though they last billions of years, they too are in process. They have their beginnings and their endings; they expand and shrink; they are younger and older, intensely bright or descending toward darkness. My experience of time seems to emanate from the immediate awareness I have of my own synthesized yet never achieved temporal totality.

The following reflections are based on a subjective exploration of my experiences of time. What is revealed to me is that my human temporality is explored and extended in movement experiences, and that the exploration and extension of myself are an important source for the meaning I find in moving. No claims are made that everyone has significant temporal experiences in movement, although it is possible because time is a variable of movement. Nor do I claim that temporal experiences are as significant for others as they are for me, although it is possible that others periodically experience the significance of their own temporality.

Time is everywhere yet nowhere. It is as straightforward as a clock yet as paradoxical as relativity. It is the most immaterial thing I know, and without it the material does not matter. It is something, yet of itself nothing. Certain considerations make me suspect that it does not exist at all or at best in a rather obscure way, because part

157

of it has gone and is no longer, and part is still to come and is not yet. A thing composed of nonexistent parts can hardly seem to deserve the name existent. However, I both have an experiential awareness of time and know of the objective structure of time in the universe.

As a temporal being I live in the now, in each new emergent now. I have lived through the past, and expect to live into the future. I am aware of my duration from moment to moment, but it is only in the present that I can think and do, only in the present can things happen to me. I cannot feel past pains or enjoy future pleasures, although the memory of past pains may affect present feelings, and the anticipation of future pleasures may give some present enjoyment. The present is the time of living and the time of either remembering past living or preparing for future living. The present is my synthesized temporality.

Aside from my own temporality, my actual perception of time as an aspect of daily living is a complex process dominated by my rhythm of attention and undoubtedly was acquired by learning. Although it is possible that there are physiological correlates of my experience of time, my temporal perception seems to rise from my experience and, as such, is subject to variations owing to, for example, nostalgia, joy, hope, pain, and memory.

My conceptual analysis of time, objectively valid as it may be, seems to be quite estranged from my subjective perspective of my experience of time. What is logically clear and valid seems perceptually false and often meaningless. So wide is the gap between these two analyses of time that each seems quite irrelevant to the other, although I am both familiar with and dependent on each system. Time as I perceive it has a crucial significance for life in general, whereas my conceptual analysis of time seems to disregard this significant connection. For example, perceptual time and conceptual time are not always alike in their characteristics. Time as I perceive it is always limited. I never perceive the whole of time; it is sensibly continuous, having a certain directional quality; it is transitive and related in its content to the subject at the moment of experience. However, time as conceived is unlimited in character, is regarded as infinitely divisible and mathematically continuous as an infinite series; it is conceived as involving an objective before-and-after order, which is not equated with the past, present, or future of my experience. Time as experienced exhibits the quality of subjective relativity, or is characterized by some sort of unequal distribution, irregularity, and nonuniformity in my personal metric. This quality differs radically from the regular, uniform, quantitative units characteristic of clock and calendar time. Memory and expectation seem to introduce a basis for distinguishing between early and late, but these distinctions will not do for an objective ordering of time. Memory and expectation are proverbially vague and fallible. They are vague in that they often fuse and overlap even in the present. They are fallible because of a number of psychological mechanisms such as forgetting, repressing, distorting, or projecting.

The theory of relativity indicates that space and time cannot be considered independently but are superseded by space-time. Accordingly, the study of the physical world is one involving a four-dimensional continuum; three of the dimensions being spatial and the fourth temporal. However, although recognizing the interdependence of time and spatial dimensions, I experience distinctive characteristics of *time* in the forms of becoming or happening and past, present, and future. Time seems to be an illusive concept. Unlike space, which has generally seemed simple and obvious to me, time is a subject of speculation, fundamentally enigmatic, even incomprehensible. Although I am rooted in space, my memory and expectation enable me in a sense to encompass time, and thus save me from being merely rooted in it.

With my concept of time as an objective structure of temporal relations in nature, I attempt to preserve my perspective of experienced time, which originates with the unidimensional character of my own life. As such, my concept of time, of instants before and after, of continuum and the like, becomes a schematic relationship of units into which my experiences can be specified. This unidimensional character of time is of value to me because it defines my existence. I do not live apart from time, but within it, a kind of plural identity of one essence.

Temporal experiences as such are basic to my consciousness of self-identity. Memory, as one form of temporal experience, is the means by which my vanished past survives within me. A temporal perspective for future allows for hope, expectation, and anticipation, involving imagination and purpose. Furthermore, my experiences of duration and sequence allow me to assign places for all events and happenings within the context of a diary of personal and social history. Thus, the significance I attribute to my temporality stems from the most simple and egocentric percept, as well as from a complex abstraction unifying past, present, and future into my being.

Experiences in movement contribute to and confuse my perceptions of time and my temporality. Both the contributions and the confusions reinforce the significance I assign to temporal experiences in movement. I acknowledge that experiences are significant only in reflection and not in action. Significance exists, in a sense, during the movement experience, but it is implicit and incomplete until reflection formalizes the meanings.

Although every conscious experience reveals a situational dependence on an attitude toward the environment, when I experience movement I am more than ever aware of my moment-to-moment existence in this world. Moving provides me with a somewhat passionate awareness of personal contingency. I feel a moment-to-moment, movement-to-movement awareness of myself in relation to the environment. The moment experienced in movement distinguishes itself by a peculiarity, a uniqueness that can neither be more fully elucidated nor further reduced. It is unique. This singularity permeates the experience of the movement which existed "in" it. I have never had this movement experience before and will never have it again. Time confines the existence of the particular movement experience to one occurrence, one moment.

Intense involvement in the movement experience provides for a relationship of simultaneity among past, present, and future. When I move there is no conscious planning for the future or reflecting on the past. There is no decision making and, perhaps, no intellectual process unrelated to my interpretation of sensation. There is an integration of all things and events. I am not separate from but with; I do not fight time, cover space, or exert force. I am all of these. I do not think, then feel or vice versa. There is simultaneity. I am. I am more than when I stop moving and begin thinking, feeling, deciding, choosing, and the like. What I experience within me is a flow, a flow that has always been going on, a flow that can be conceived of as an intentional arc uniting the past of myself with the future of who I will be. Movement is a temporal catalyst of and between my selves. There always is this concretely present flow of past and future in the present, in the now of intending the completion of the move. If unity can be conceived of as a process instead of a static state, I experience the now of moving as a unity of succession. How I begin the move, the process of doing the move, the way I end the move, and the result of the move are all one, defining that move and me as complete temporal wholes.

My experiences in movement are characterized by successive temporal wholes and also by something which endures within succession. This experience of continuance from one present to another is the experience of duration. The duration of a temporal whole varies with the particular movement experience. My experience of the tennis serve has a different duration from my experience of the tennis game, yet each is experienced as a temporal whole extending from beginning to ending, and distinct from the present occupied by the tennis match. The duration of temporal wholes is distinguished by pauses in or rests from movement.

While moving I often become so absorbed in the task that duration is interrupted. In a swimming race I may hear the starting gun and then realize that I am swimming my second stroke. I find myself swaying during a difficult stunt on the balance beam, and then suddenly find myself into the next move. In neither case is there any definite consciousness of what happened during the brief period of time, but time did not drop out of existence, duration did not stop. On the contrary, it presents me with a peculiar quality of experienced duration quite divorced from the ordinary measure of time.

Even without exact measurements it is common for time to appear to vary in duration according to the nature of the movement experience. The experience of the last minute of the game varies greatly in duration, depending on whether the score is tied or quite one sided. Also familiar to me are those movement experiences which through intense involvement in the experience provide for a feeling of timelessness or eternalness, a suspension of duration in which time does not start and stop but holds the moment. This feeling of extended temporality is exhilarating in both action and reflection.

From my perception of my body, now at this point, now at that point, comes the realization that movement is taking place. However, in this realization I have numbered the two nows and recognized that time has passed. Just as movement is recognized from perceiving the moving body at two different places, so time is recognized by me from perceiving the two nows, or the same now entering into two different relations, one before, one after. The dependence of the time–space continuum on the experience of movement leads me to believe that there is also a spatial unity in the experience of movement—a here-to-here experience of self which can be distinguished only through language from the moment-to-moment experience of self.

Although the relationship of time and space dependency is always evident in abstractions about movement experiences, I often experience time as an independent variable in movement.

For example, there are many instances in movement when a sudden move means the difference between beating or being beaten by an opponent on the take-off, reaching a ball that otherwise would have been just out of reach, and regaining or losing balance. I recognize the necessity of a spatial dimension in each of the examples, but I may experience the temporal necessity to the exclusion of the spatial.

In many movement activities the faster movement is the better or more skillful movement. Speed is often of more interest to me than slow movements or movements of spatial accuracy. On the other hand, I have experienced doing a movement too quickly. There is not an automatic challenge for me to accomplish a movement in the most appropriate time. Timing, as I experience it in my performance, is a synchronization of my internalization of time with the externalization of movement.

Other temporal challenges for me in movement involve identifying the rhythm or cadence of particular movement activities. Is the rhythm definite and imposed? Is there a predetermined order into which I establish rhythm? Can I establish my rhythm or must I move in relation to another's rhythm? Does the rhythm of the movement change from person to person or team to team? I wonder also whether I enjoy endurance activities more as I grow older because they offer me the challenge of a relentless time?

Temporal experiences permeate my experiences in movement. From the decision to take time to play or move, the separation of my work and play experiences according to time, to the completion of the last movement and often beyond the act to the completion of the experience of the movement, is part of my experience. Time not only designs the movements but also is significant in my understanding of my movement experience. Of all the ways that time contributes to and confuses my experiences in movement the most significant temporal experiences are those moments in movement when unity of self, of who I was, am, and will be, and the unity of time, past, present, and future, before, now, and after, are experienced as one—when my temporality is at once extended and understood, when the singularity of that moment in time is united with the simultaneity of my experience of self.

Chapter 20

Sexuality and Sport

Bonnie A. Beck

> *The life instinct, or sexual instinct, demands activity of a kind that, in contrast to our current mode of activity, can only be called play. The life instinct ... demands union with others and with the world around us based not on anxiety and aggression but on narcissism and erotic exuberance.*[6]

The life instinct demands an acceptance of "Soma," or "Me, the Bodily Being."[1] The recognition and respect for ourselves as sexual beings enable us to authentically attend to our inner reality and to spontaneously and uninhibitedly act on it. When cognizant of our sexuality, our bodily signals and our pulsating sensual-sexual responses become guideposts for authentic action. Choices for action reflect creativity, and our uniqueness of being is a blend and flow of full human sexuality, not shackled or bound by crippling social expectations.

Stanley Keleman proclaimed:

> *Very few people want to accept the flat statement that we are sexual organisms, that we are alive basically in a sexual way. ... People are willing to make all kinds of other trips: we are religious beings with a sexual function; we are political-economic beings with a sexual function; we are a humanistic organism that has a sexual part. It's very elaborate, intricate and sometimes quite beautiful thinking, but ... it avoids the truth: that fundamentally we are sexual beings, and we live sexual lives on one level or another, and to the degree that our sexuality is not fulfilled, we are crippled.*[3]

The life instinct, our playful, sexual nature, authentically demands an embracing of life and urges an unabashed, unashamed polysexual engagement with the world in which we live. The life instinct prompts a negation of the traditionally masculine or the traditionally feminine role we have learned to play and urges an emergence of our inner, nondichotomized sexual reality. The life instinct seeks a removal of all arbitrarily defined sexual inhibitions and calls on all human beings to rejoice in the freedom of their feminine-masculine unity.

Sports, ideally, offer the opportunity for both women and men to call attention to their identity and sexual unity as whole persons as they "stand naked before the gods and other persons to testify to the extent of their own personal powers."[2] The opportunity to engage other somas, in the spirit of Patroclus, in an effort to exalt and discover the ultimate potentiality of males, of females, and of all human beings has been the beauty and the challenge of sports for generations.

The playgrounds of life, especially those accommodating sports, have offered the potential promise of personal excellence and the sanction of authentic human expression. Sports have spoken, perhaps covertly, to the opportunity for individuals to unify themselves in the orgasmic explosion of carnal pleasure which results from somas meeting somas in authentic mutuality in an atmosphere divorced from stifling, crippling social conventionality.

The games of skill, chance, competition, and sensate intrigue have, since time immemorial, titillated the life instinct of many, and drawn young and old, female and male, to explore firsthand or vicariously the pleasures contained in a body eroticized and balanced through motion. Sports, as depicted in the media, and as sometimes played in society, suggest to women and men that on the fields of play childlike exuberance, spontaneous expression, and celebration of bodily pleasures are the rule rather than the exception.

The traditional lascivious connotations surrounding the pursuit and public expression of carnal pleasure that were reinforced and maintained through our Christian heritage are negated during the course of play. Sports create the aura of human intimacy wherein the public expression of love of man for man and woman for woman is sanctioned and ennobled. Young men and young women after a hard-won victory enthusiastically reach for one another and spin around and around in their joy. Their actions know no social limitations and their inner reality, their authentic sexuality, makes them whole and they are momentarily reborn. Their human sexuality, that is, their capacity for union with one another, is fulfilled, not in anxiety and aggression, but in narcissism and erotic exuberance.[6]

With the idealized illusion that sports may, in fact, provide for the expression of man's life instinct, the questions must be asked: In what ways *do* contemporary sports as organized and played limit or extend the human quest for discovery, acceptance, and celebration of human pleasure and sexual authenticity? In what ways do sports facilitate the development of unique individuals and in what ways do they create female and male automatons?

The answers to the aforementioned questions must be sought in a mold of other questions: (1) Will the experiences found in sports be bounded by socially contrived, artificially prescribed female-based and male-based conformity, or will sports provide for creative, innovative participation based on the needs and desires of individuals? (2) Will the participants be asked to involve themselves in the game in a mechanistic fashion, or will they be encouraged to explore the essence of the sports experience?

Sports participation, as well as all other facets of life, offers the potential for human pleasure and the authenticity of sexual expression. Whether or not this potential is realized often depends on the prescribed or selected modes of personal involvement. The following possibilities for involvement in sports may offer a yardstick by which to measure the ultimate human benefits and suggest some answers to the questions asked previously.

Sports, through their organizational structure and social function, may direct the participation of individuals toward an *objective-performance* level of involvement. Individuals engaged in sports at this level are involved in the *act* of sport, wherein their *act*ions are public and subject to scrutiny and judgments by standards external to them. Attention is called to the special skills of the performer, and assessment of these skills is made apart from the feelings the actions precipitated in the performer. Patsy Neal wrote of this concept of involvement:

> *Does it seem strange that we watch plays on stage, and that we watch athletes play at sports? They are both performances. They both have actors playing at the real thing, and trying to become involved to such a degree that their actions become perfected and authentic. Players "suit up" for their performances, while actors "dress up." . . . Everyone plays his role, but what part is a role, and what part is real?*[5]

Sports participation becomes an *act* when the actions of the performer and the outcome of the performance are intended for public rather than private consumption. This level of involvement could be called "sport for the other." This is not to deny that pleasure does not accrue for the participant, it is only that pleasure is a concomitant of the external rewards, that is, the thunderous roar of the crowd, hero-status, scholarships, privileged status-on-campus, and the like.

The objective-performance dimension of sports participation perpetuates one of the socially prescribed functions of sports, namely, the socialization of young men (and women, only recently, if at all) into responsible, socially productive, mature men (and women). From this perspective, task assignation relative to biological sex as reflected in the movement patterns known as football, modern dance, and the like, heightens and welds into the social consciousness prescriptions for human conformity. The bifurcated participation of individuals along sex-differentiated lines creates a drama based on masculine and feminine idealism. Character actors (male athletes) and actresses (cheerleaders) play in full view to the thousands who come to cheer their football hero and his homecoming queen.

The sports experience for women and men, girls and boys, could take another tack, however, toward a more *subjective-intuitive-personal* mode of involvement. Within this realm of participation, the skills, feelings, desires, and expressions of the participants would be private and subject only to personal scrutiny. The motivation for entering the game would be intrinsic to the player and would not depend on the second hand of the stopwatch or the tumultuous roar of the crowd.

The *subjective-personal* mode of involvement in sports returns the game to the players. Role definitions for females and males are blurred as men, women, and children, both young and old, seek to become and are welcomed as participants. Sports, in this modality, are for the person, an avenue for creative human expression, not bounded by rules designed to make the game understandable to the public.

Sports, as currently played in schools, colleges, Pop Warner Leagues, Little Leagues, and professionally, usually focus on the *objective act* of participation or involvement. The emphasis is on *beating the opponents,* and this end defines the rather narrow means required for attainment of the objective. Winning, being *number one*, requires that some players "sit the bench" for most of the season and ensures that others, less skilled, never make the team at all. Women, and most men, are denied the traditional pinnacles *(crème de la crème)* of sports involvement because of the tunneling effect of social prescription, which mandates that only the fittest of males ever reach the top.

Sports, as organized in the United States, appear to be energized by forces that take no cognizance of the life instinct of the human beings they are intended to serve. The limitation imposed by our traditional concept of sports for males only (and a few "strange" females) has negated the idealized concept of sports wherein every woman and man could stand naked before the gods and others to demonstrate and prove their personal powers.[2]

When sport involvement is limited artificially by one's biological sex, then it seems imperative that we examine, in light of the life instinct, the price that both women and men must pay for the illogical restriction. Those individuals responsible for the management of sports—the coaches, teachers, officials, players, and spectators—must recognize their contributions to the perpetuation of sexually crippled women and men. The acceptance of this conclusion will facilitate a reordering of the sports experience to enhance the sexual freedom of all who enter the door marked Sports.

The sports experience holds much glamor and allure for young boys and girls in the United States. A brief glimpse into the structure of this experience may assist in the process of redefining priorities for sport participation.

Young boys, drawn by the intrigue of the playground and the sport found there, learn firsthand and quite early that lesson number one is that girls are inferior to boys. Adult, peer, and parental pressure combine to reinforce in the young boy that he is to repress (at the ultimate expense of his full sexuality) any sign of socially defined feminine behaviors in himself. He learns that the "real sports" are for *males only,* and to be accepted fully into the "sports fraternity," he must always be fully prepared to play his role as defined for him on the fields of play.

The first lesson that association with sports teaches the young boy is a lesson in repression and denial; a lesson that will ultimately "make foreign" and fragment his sexual reality. He quickly learns through his involvement in sports to attend only to those bodily signals which he identifies (or have been identified for him) as masculine and, over time, those will be the only ones he knows. The young boy learns to *act* like a man rather than just to *be* one.

In this society males more often than females are denied the freedom to explore their sexual authenticity. The connotations suggested by the word "sissy" carry far greater social and personal repercussions for the young boy, to whom the word is directed, than does the word "tomboy" for his sister.

Men learn not to cry or to show other visible signs of weakness when hurt, fearful, or disappointed. In sports, however, men do learn that it is socially appropriate to cry with "real men," that is, with their teammates of the locker-room fraternity. Yet, crying in front of women and children is still considered a sign of weakness, a loss of masculinity. Men's "inner watch-dog" must be busy indeed, attempting to discern when certain bodily signals will be attended to and when they will not be.

Men, encouraged and well-applauded in the sports world, in their race to capture the aura of Phallus-Erectus-Non-Interruptus and all that the concept entails, lose in their blind end-run their inherently bisexual nature. Their personal balance, the blend of soft-hard, passive-aggressive, open-closed, and dependent-independent, is disrupted and the result becomes a cookie-cutter mold, inflexible and rigid, capable only of stamping out hard, aggressive, closed, independent, sexually crippled men of the future.

Human individuality, uniqueness of being, potential balance, and unity of the whole person, as ideally or hopefully sought in sports, are lost. The opportunity for union of the man-boy with himself is diminished, and the potentiality for realizing the life instinct, the playful, sexually authentic nature of the male human being is stunted, stifled, and denied.

The life instinct speaks to young girls no less than to young boys, in urging an active, personal, intimate engagement in life. Girls, too, harken to the intrigue of the playground in an effort to meet the challenges of the games. Young girls seek, also, to "stand naked before the gods and other human beings to testify to the extent of their own personal powers."[2]

Girls and women seek sports in an attempt to discover firsthand their boundaries. They come to the playing fields, pools, and courts to ascertain how fast they can run, how far they can throw, how much they can lift, who they can defeat, and in what sports and by whom they can be defeated. Young girls are attracted to sports for the same reasons that are young boys. Their bodies, their life instinct, and their authentic sexuality tell them they must.

And what opportunities in sport await a girl's youthful enthusiasm? What liberating, boundary-identifying, life-giving experiences behold her as she spontaneously bursts on the scene with a "Hey, can I play?"

Sports, she will soon learn, demand little of her. Sports for women, although rapidly becoming more acceptable, remain an anathema to pictorialized femininity. *Serious* involvement in sport, that is, the provision of expert coaching, social-parental applause, on-par facilities and equipment, and concomitant support services, has yet to be realized for girls and women in sports. Whereas there is usually ample funding for cheerleaders and majorettes, funding of sports for girls and women in most schools and colleges (to say nothing of professional leagues) is the dregs from the bottom of the barrel.

A young girl's joy and enthusiasm for sports is usually short-lived, as the social message rapidly reminds her that the preferred role for girls and women continues to be that of a support and an accessory figure to the male. She learns that her primary role in life, that of wife and mother, is not enhanced through skills acquired on the playing fields, that, in fact, continued and serious involvement in sports may even be a detriment to marriage and motherhood.

The young girl quickly learns, as did her brother, that to step from the role ascribed to her by society and enforced in the domain of sport is to invite covert and overt social reprimands, not the least of which being suggested gender-role aberration. Women and girls seriously engaged in sports have had to bear the stigma of sexual deviancy, a crown of thorns which few have elected to wear.

There is much support, as reflected in the current opposition to the Title IX guidelines, for the proposition that society, to date, does not value excellence in sports for women in the same way that it values excellence in sports for men. Social acceptance and reward for women standing shoulder to shoulder with men on the playing fields have yet to be realized, and there is continued resistance from both women and men to the full and unqualified participation of girls and women in sports.

To the degree that participation in sports is limited to "only males" or "only females," or the movement patterns within the sports are prescribed by the polarizing and fragmenting molds of "flexibility for females" and "muscularity for males," it will not be possible for women or men to experience the full extent of their human sexuality. Sports, to liberate the essence of being fully human, must provide for nonsexually based participation and permit creative human expression and movement patterns rather than staid, mechanistic movements derived from archaic masculine and feminine patterns.

The quest for human freedom in sports participation appears to be founded in two dimensions of sport: (1) the organizational structure of the sport, and (2) the sexual makeup of the teams, or who will be permitted to play? To date, sports as we know them have perpetuated a militaristic, capitalistic society. They have been exclusively male-oriented and as such have reflected a masculinized society.

Each year sports become more and more competitive, more and more exclusive, and more and more hierarchical. Traditional sports appear to be locked into a never-ending, upward spiral, a funnel destined to carry the seeds of its own destruction. George Leonard questioned the legitimacy of maintaining our present sports structure and model for participation.

> ... *let's ask how much more we need to encourage aggression and territorial war (football), relentless fakery (basketball) and obsession with records (baseball). It's a fundamental law of evolution that the final period in any line of development is marked by grotesqueries and extremes. The widespread glorification of winning at all costs reached its height during a war this nation did not win. Hyped-up sports metaphor—"game plans," "enemy lists" and the like—came to pre-occupy a national Administration just before that game was up.*[4]

In light of Leonard's remarks, the question of extremes, of the traditionally rigid social prescriptions for male behaviors and female behaviors, for winning at any cost, and for objectifying subjective phenomenon, prompts the suggestion that perhaps we are on the edge of a new era. Perhaps we are embarking on a "somatic revolution"[1] which will exalt, glorify, and celebrate the life instinct in both women and men. Guides for this new era may be few and widely dispersed. It would behoove us, however, to look to established sages in an effort to discern viable directions.

One such direction might be found in the Chinese philosophy which utilizes the characters of Yin and Yang to note the blend and flow of polar opposites. Yin is the negative, dark, and feminine principle and Yang is the bright, positive, and masculine principle. It is, however, the interaction of these two characters which influences the destinies and realities of all creatures and things. The Yin and Yang, in flow, occur within us all, and it is the appearance of first one, then the other, which speaks to the recognition of authentic sexuality and sets the stage for lives marked by pleasure and spontaneity rather than lives of guilt and fragmentation.

Americans have failed, to date, to accommodate, recognize, or reward the possibility of both Yin and Yang residing in both women and men. Rather, as a people we have spoken in linear terms with value judgments being cast on the spectrum. Americans have said that it is *better* for males to be only masculine, rather than masculine and feminine, and that it is better for females to be only feminine rather than both feminine and masculine.

Americans have viewed sexually inappropriate behaviors as sexually deviant behaviors, and males who expressed gentleness and aesthetic qualities, rather than assertive, independent qualities, were often called sissy and effeminate, and social aspersions were cast on their manhood and attendant heterosexuality. Sports were often the testing ground for boys about to become men. One wonders of the price paid by those boys-men who did not make it.

The linear comparison of polarities, of femaleness and maleness, has created fragmentation and guilt among women and men who do not fit so neatly into the prescribed box. Coveting of opposite-sex characteristics often leaves women and men shaken, unsure of their own gender identity.

The ancient model provided by the characters of Yin and Yang would enable all of us, female and male, young and old, participant, and nonparticipant, to accommodate and joyously express the gamut of human sexuality. As a woman, I would be encouraged to recognize and accept within myself my potential for being both feminine and masculine. With this freedom, perhaps our behaviors would not be so skewed along sexually crippling lines.

Old patterns, concepts, folkways, and beliefs die hard, and the transition from the traditional sport forms to new forms and patterns of participation will not happen over night. However, some people, institutions, and organizations in the United States are beginning to offer new models for the organization of and participation in sports.

A few of the signs pointing toward a refocusing of the sports experience for women and men may be found in recent federal legislation, namely, Title IX of the Educational Amendments Act. The intended consequences of this Act are full and equal opportunities for women and men to participate together in the sport of their choice. This legislation requires that the old mechanistic traditions of football for males and dance for females fall by the wayside.

Another hint of the potential dissolution of our contemporary mode of sports organization and participation is found in the

emergence of organizations such as the Sports Center at the Esalen
Institute in San Francisco, California. Classes offered at the Sports
Center are designed to celebrate human playfulness, joyfulness,
and authentic human sexuality.

Examples of the new courses offered at Esalen are "Sensory
Awareness in Sports," "Body Flying," and "The Arts of Unwind-
ing." The focus is *subjective-personal-experiential*. Participation is
based on desire, and inclusion rather than exclusion is the mode.
Participants are urged to seek their own excellence through
creative motion.

Following the Esalen example, in October of 1973 in a small
valley in Merin County, California, over 5,000 women, men, and
children attended the first New Games Tournament.[4] The theory of
New Games, as explained by Stewart Brand, publisher of the
Whole Earth Catalog, is:

> *You can't change the game by winning it, losing
> it, refereeing it or spectating it. You can change the
> game by leaving it. Then you can start a new game. If
> it has its own strength and appeal, it may survive.
> Most likely it won't. In either case, you will have
> learned something about the process of game-
> changing and the particular limitations imposed on
> us by certain games.*[4]

If we are on the edge of a "somatic revolution"[4] and sports are
to be a part of the movement toward human liberation, then the
form and substance of sports must change. It will not be enough for
the traditional sports to be opened to women, although of course
they must. It will not be enough for institutions to provide separate
but equal sports experiences for females and males, although there
will be many who use this as a first step. It is not enough for women
and men to stand shoulder to shoulder on the playing fields, if those
who control the games that they play refuse to recognize, exalt, and
liberate the life instinct.

As women, and more men, move more fully into the totality of
sport, their contributions must be to the celebration of the life
instinct of the participants. Women and men must work to eradicate
the basis of sexual discrimination which is founded in the
paternalistic, mechanistic structure of sports.

Cultural laws are often enforced many years before attitudinal
changes occur. Today, we have the laws that urge us to move off a
sex-differentiated, discriminatory base. Personal feelings, attitudes,

and beliefs held concerning the "normal female" and the "normal male" continue, however, to make us hold firm to the status quo and to insist on the right of deciding what sports, movements, or games will be appropriate for women and men. We have, to date, failed to accommodate a blend of Yin and Yang within women and men.

Social comments concerning the characteristics that identify and differentiate females from males will be with us for many years. Sport as a dominant force in the maintenance and perpetuation of the socially based stereotypes of a "manly man" and a "womanly woman" will not easily succumb to alternative models. Yet, change is written on the wind, so succumb it must.

Those involved in sports, as participants, coaches, administrators, observers, must recognize the presence of the life instinct and move to accommodate this energy for living within the structure of sport. Sports must accept, exalt, and encourage "Soma, Me the Bodily Being,"[1] a unified, strong, balanced and vital individual, who is ready, eager, and capable of meeting other "somas" in the spirit of pleasureful exuberance in quest of human excellence.

The mandate for sports participation and organization must be based on women and men meeting one another in the spirit of idealized sport. Sports must provide the opportunity for women and men to "stand together, naked, on the playing fields before gods and all others to testify and celebrate the extent of their own personal powers, their own identity, their own sexuality." This is the challenge to the new era in sports, one key to the liberation of authentic human sexuality.

REFERENCES

1. Hanna, T.: *Bodies in Revolt*. New York: Dell Publishing Co., 1970.
2. Hart, M. (Ed.): *Sport in the Socio-Cultural Process*. Dubuque, Iowa: Wm. C. Brown Publishers, 1972.
3. Keleman, S.: *Sexuality, Self and Survival*. San Francisco: Lodestar Press, 1971.
4. Leonard, G.: The Games People *Should* Play. *Esquire, LXXXII:* 214–217+, 1974.
5. Neal, P.: *Sport and Identity*. Philadelphia: Dorrance and Company, 1972.
6. Roszak, T.: *Sources*. New York: Harper & Row, Publishers, 1970.

SPECIAL READING

Brown, N.: *Love's Body*. New York: Random House, Inc., 1966.
Buckley, W.: Reflections on the Phenomenon. *Esquire, LXXXII:* 125–128, 1974.
Esalen Catalog. XII: 11–14, 1974.

Huizinga, J.: *Homo Ludens.* Boston: Beacon Press, 1950.
Koestenbaum, P.: *Existential Sexuality.* Englewood Cliffs, N.J.: Prentice-Hall, Inc., 1974.
Leonard, G.: *The Transformation: A Guide to the Inevitable Changes in Humankind.*. New York: Delacorte Press, 1972.
Lowen, A.: *Pleasure.* New York: Lancer Books, Inc., 1970.
Lowen, A.: *Love and Orgasm.* New York: The Macmillan Co., 1965.
Maisel, E. (Ed.): *The Resurrection of the Body.* New York: The Dell Publishing Co., 1969.